How does the Guide work?

Under 5s

5-8 Year-olds

9-12 Year-olds

Teenagers

The Guide is divided into four colour-coded age categories for easy reference. Within each section, books are arranged in approximate age order. In addition, each book has a Reading Age (RA), indicating the suggested age necessary to read the text and an Interest Level (IL) which indicates the full age-range for which it is likely to appeal most.

Each entry includes bibliographic details for easy ordering at bookshops and libraries. All books listed are paperback unless otherwise stated.

At the end of the Guide is a title and author index, as well as a subject index, listing some of the major themes running through the books.

How are the books selected?

Booktrust receives a copy of almost every children's book published in the UK each year. This Guide features some of the outstanding titles that caught our eye throughout 2003, as well as submissions from publishers. (First paperback edition must have been published in the UK in 2003. The Guide only features picture books and fiction.)

We have an extensive team of expert reviewers, ranging from Booktrust staff to teachers, librarians, writers, parents and people from the book world. This diversity of experience and viewpoint ensures that there is something for every taste, interest and ability.

Sarah Aston
Editor

Books for the Under 5s

Books for babies should be bold, bright and colourful. The various formats available (such as bath books, cloth books and board books) can withstand lots of rough treatment and will allow babies to become familiar with the concepts of holding a book and turning the pages. These books invite the very young to touch, point out and identify familiar objects in stories and rhymes.

Pre-school children should be given books that encourage them both to discuss the story and play an active role in storytelling, as well as help them to learn words. Bright and attractive illustrations are very important. Once children begin to learn to read for themselves, they will often return to these early favourites.

Row, Row, Row Your Boat

Illustrated by Annie Kubler

Child's Play (Board Book) £3.99 ISBN: 0 85953 658 0

This well-known song is brought to life by award-winning artist Annie Kubler in another of her sturdy, colourful books, which have become firm favourites with many parents.

Actions to accompany the verses are demonstrated in lively watercolour illustrations of bright and cheerful babies, bursting with energy. They will certainly encourage young babies and toddlers to copy them and join in. The music is printed on the back cover, so there is no excuse for adult readers not to sing along!
RA 4+/IL 0-4

Maisy Likes Music

Lucy Cousins

Walker Books (Board Book) £4.99 ISBN: 0 7445 9249 6

This board book has a clear spine filled with coloured beads, so it can also be used as a rattle and shaken, in keeping with the story's musical theme.

Maisy and her familiar cast of friends are shown playing a variety of musical instruments, each of which has its own sound: 'tooty toot!', 'cha-cha cha!' At the end of the book, the friends play together in a colourful, noisy orchestra. The illustrations have a simple charm, and each onomatopoeic word has been carefully chosen. RA 4+/IL 0-4

Happy Dog Sad Dog

Sam Lloyd

Little Tiger Press (Board Book) £3.99 ISBN: 1 85430 874 2

This bright and cheerful board book won the 2003 Sainsbury's Baby Book Award. It is a great introduction to the concept of opposites for babies and toddlers and is sure to make them laugh as they learn.

In a bold palette of orange, purple, green, yellow, blue and red, Sam Lloyd paints dogs in all shapes, sizes and conditions: big, little, clean, dirty, hot, cold, awake, asleep, hairy and bald. A simple idea, wonderfully executed. RA 4+/IL 0-4

Mirror Me!

Julie Aigner-Clark, illustrated by Nadeem Zaidi

Scholastic Children's Books (Board Book) £3.99
ISBN: 0 439 97327 9

This short board book comprises six drawings of animals making faces. Opposite each animal is the same drawing, but the face is replaced by a mirror, so that babies can see themselves copying the expressions. Bard the lizard opens his eyes wide, Frog sticks out his tongue, Cow puffs his cheeks full of air, and Jane the monkey makes a silly face. Further information and ideas for parents are listed on the back of the book. A simple and fun first book for toddlers. RA 4+/IL 0-4

That's Not My Bear...

Fiona Watt, illustrated by Rachel Wells

Usborne (Board Book) £4.99 ISBN: 0 7460 5159 X

A different bear is introduced on each page of this colourful board book, but there is something not quite right about most of them: one's nose is too rough, another's paws are too soft, and one's tongue is too scratchy.

Babies will enjoy hearing the repetitive chant of 'that's not my bear', and will be delighted when, on the final page, the right bear is found. With bold, vibrant illustrations and a variety of interesting textures throughout, this touchy-feely board book is ideal for inquisitive babies and toddlers. RA 4+/IL 0-4

One Gorgeous Baby

Martine Oborne, illustrated by Ingrid Goden

Macmillan Children's Books £4.99 ISBN: 0 333 96038 6

This picture book, which simply oozes love, accompanies one gorgeous baby on its daily journey from breakfast to bedtime. Each of the ten scenes is full of things to count and noises to make.

The illustrations are gentle and uncomplicated and the softly-diffused colours bring a delightful warmth to the pages. This book is a comfort blanket from start to finish. RA 4+/IL 0-5

Babies

Ros Asquith, illustrated by Sam Williams

Macmillan Children's Books £4.99 ISBN: 0 333 96394 6

This irresistible picture book gives the low-down on babies and the antics they get up to every day. There are big babies and little babies; babies who like teddies, muddles and bathtimes; bouncy babies and a baby who plays with the honey jar; angry babies and do-little babies.

Every page of this delightful and happy book will bring a smile of recognition to anyone who has ever been near a baby. A mirror page at the end of the book gives babies the chance to look at themselves. Absolutely adorable. RA 5+/IL 0-5

A Time For Everything

Susie Poole

Pupfish (Board Book) £4.99 ISBN: 1 904637 01 9

This beautifully illustrated little book gently teaches very young children about the variety to be found in life's experiences: happiness and sadness; hellos and goodbyes; noisiness and quiet; waking up and going to sleep; getting grubby and cleaning up; loving and being loved. In busy young lives there really is 'a time for everything'.

The jolly pictures of lively children in this charming and robust board book will appeal to a wide range of young readers. RA 5+/IL 2-4

I Know a Rhino

Charles Fuge

Gullane Children's Books (Board Book) £3.99
ISBN: 1 86233 523 0

The energetic toddler in this captivating board book knows lots of larger-than-life animals, with whom she has a variety of adventures. Whether she is taking tea with a rhino or blowing bubbles with a giraffe in the bath, the little girl's imagination runs riot in glorious colour.

Eventually, the mismatched menagerie of hippo, leopard, ape, pig and dragon troops upstairs to bed, where they become comforting soft-toy friends. The sprightly illustrations are accompanied by simple, rhyming text that is a joy to read aloud. RA 5+/IL 1-5

This Little Chick

John Lawrence

Walker Books £4.99 ISBN: 0 7445 9479 0

Little Chick visits a variety of farmyard animals and learns the different noises they make. By the time he returns to his mother and siblings he can repeat them all.

The rhyming text in this wonderful book for the very young moves along in a bouncy, cheerful manner, and the accompanying woodcut illustrations are simply stunning. A lovely book for small children and adults to enjoy together. RA 5+/IL 2-5

Postman Bear

Julia Donaldson,
illustrated by Axel Scheffler

Macmillan Children's Books £4.99 ISBN: 0 333 96624 4

The highly successful Donaldson/Scheffler partnership has produced another perfect read for the under fives.

Postman Bear writes three letters and goes out to deliver them in Acorn Wood. By lifting the flaps young readers can find out who they are for (Frog, Squirrel and Mole) and see that they are actually invitations to Bear's party. Axel Scheffler's illustrations are large, colourful and enjoyably detailed. RA 5+/IL 2-5

No Matter What

Debi Gliori

Bloomsbury Children's Books £5.99 ISBN: 0 7475 6331 4

This touching tale about two foxes explores the unconditional love a parent has for a child. When Small questions the extent of Large's love – 'But if I turned into a bug, would you still love me and give me a hug?'– Large swiftly responds with reassuring answers. Large even has a satisfying reply to Small's difficult question: 'But what about when we're dead and gone?'

The repetitive, rhyming text is accompanied by warm, vibrant illustrations. Young children will love joining in with the chant, 'I'll always love you, no matter what'.
RA 6+/IL 2-6

Bedtime Little Monsters

Emma Harris, illustrated by Paul Cherrill

Little Tiger Press £4.99 ISBN: 1 85430 837 8

Lift-the-flap books are hugely popular with the very young, who love the secrets and the surprises – and the participation. This is a bedtime story that children will relate to, for the Little Monsters simply do not want to go to bed!

The short, rhyming text has real child-appeal and contains tempting words for the listener to join in with as they lift the flaps and discover the hidden monsters (all of which are different colours). RA 5+/IL 3-6

Smile, Crocodile, Smile

An Vrombaut

Oxford University Press £4.99 ISBN: 0 19 272547 5

It's time to wake up at the Mango Tree House and Crocodile and her friends must brush their teeth before the day's activities begin. However it takes Crocodile so long to brush all her teeth that she misses out on all the fun with her friends.

This vibrant and colourful story humorously introduces themes of friendship and consideration for others. RA 6+/IL 3-6

Let's Play Fairies!

Sue Heap

Walker Books £4.99 ISBN: 0 7445 9497 9

Lily May wants to play fairies, but her friends each want to play their own game: trees, cars, cats, even wibbly-wobbly jellies. They play each game in turn, Lily May quietly suggesting 'fairies' every time, then equally quietly joining in with the others when a noisier game is chosen. At last, when they agree that her magic wand will allow them to fly, they play fairies and find it great fun.

Pictures and text unite perfectly in this thoughtful, funny and salutary book. RA 5+/IL 2-6

Can I Play?

Janet Thomas, illustrated by Alison Bartlett

Egmont £4.99 ISBN: 1 4052 0597 0

Casper Cat wants to play 'tig' with his best friend Susie Sheep, but Milly Goat comes along and takes Susie away. Casper feels excluded and has to content himself with watching them play. When Casper's mum takes him to the park, he realises that it is possible to play 'tig' in a group. Mum encourages Casper to stand up for himself, so that the next time Milly ignores him he has the perfect reply at the ready.

This is a colourful book that deals sensitively with a difficult issue. RA 5+/IL 2-6

Chimp and Zee

Catherine and Laurence Anholt

Frances Lincoln £5.99 ISBN: 0 7112 2121 9

This is another winning offering from the much-loved Anholt partnership. Chimp and Zee, the naughty, lovable monkey twins, like to hide in the banana basket and play tricks on Mumkey. On a shopping trip to town they settle down in the basket on one of three grey stones while Mumkey does the shopping. But when the three grey stones turn out to be three grey elephants who suddenly move off into the deepest, darkest part of Jungletown taking the basket with them, what will happen to Chimp and Zee?

Delightfully told, with fabulously-detailed, colourful illustrations executed in classic Anholt style, this is sure to become a bedtime favourite! RA 5+/IL 2-6

Snow Bears

Martin Waddell,
illustrated by Sarah Fox-Davies

Walker Books £4.99 ISBN: 0 7445 9488 X

This gentle, very beautiful picture book is about three baby bears playing in the snow with their mummy; they play together, hiding, sliding and throwing snowballs, until they get cold and go home. When the snow on their fur melts, the snow bears become Mummy Bear's baby bears again.

This warm story, with Sarah Fox-Davies's wonderful illustrations, is a delight. RA 7+/IL 2-6

Sleepy Pendoodle

Malachy Doyle, illustrated by Julie Vivas

Walker Books £4.99 ISBN: 0 7445 9477 4

A little girl finds a lost puppy, but in spite of all her efforts he refuses to open his eyes. Finally, he wakes up, and proves to be a joyously lively character – every child's idea of a perfect play companion.

With its clear, crisp layout and colourful illustrations, this is a great book for reading and sharing. The simple language and happy subject matter make it ideal for repeated bedtime readings. RA 5+/IL 2-6

Pizza Kittens

Charlotte Voake

Walker Books £5.99 ISBN: 0 7445 9810 9

Lucy, Joe and Bert are kittens who behave just like most small children: they watch too much TV, hate vegetables, prefer squash to water, and, unless it's pizza, spread their meals around the kitchen. Their parents struggle in vain to introduce vegetables into the family's diet, until Dad compromises by cooking pizza ... with a side salad!

Energetic pictures of domestic non-bliss, large-print text and a satisfyingly realistic outcome ensure that this will be a hit with children of all ages. Winner of the 2002 Nestlé Smarties Book Prize Silver Medal. RA 6+/IL 2-6

Treasure Hunt

Allan Ahlberg, illustrated by Gillian Tyler

Walker Books £4.99 ISBN: 0 7445 9495 2

Ordinary family life is transformed into a series of small adventures in this wonderful picture book. Tilly is a curious toddler who loves treasure hunting; her parents obligingly hide small 'treasures' – a banana, her rabbit, even themselves – so that she can search for them.

With deft use of rhythm and repetition, the story reaches its charming bedtime conclusion, in which the tables are turned and it's Tilly who hides. The gentle, atmospheric illustrations convey the seasons and domestic routines with energy, humour and wonderful warmth. RA 5+/IL 3-6

Sleep Tight, Baboon Bear

Bette Westera,
illustrated by Suzanne Diederen
Allen & Unwin £4.99 ISBN: 1 86508 773 4

This is a charming bedtime story, which focuses on the fears of a child spending his first night away from home.

William Walter and Baboon Bear are going to stay the night with Oma Annie. William Walter is fine but Baboon Bear is uneasy: he dawdles for the bus, mopes in the doorway instead of playing in the garden, doesn't enjoy his dinner and can't sleep for the long-haired shadows on the wall.

Baboon does eventually find comfort but the real joy of this book lies in Suzanne Diederen's exquisitely-realised and instantly appealing illustrations, which bring William Walter and, most of all, Baboon Bear to life. RA 6+/IL 3-6

I Want to be a Cowgirl

Jeanne Willis, illustrated by Tony Ross
Andersen Press £4.99 ISBN: 1 84270 308 0

The determined heroine of this magical picture book knows exactly what she wants. She rejects 'girly' behaviour, the classroom and books – and even the big city is too small for her huge dreams.

She yearns for the Wild, Wild West, and has the spurs and lasso to prove it; she even practises her cowgirl moves with a stray dog in the old scrapyard. Even the view from the twentieth floor of a high-rise block can't dampen her spirits, so that, eventually, long-suffering Daddy throws off his city clothes and runs off to the Wild West too.

An irresistible rhyming text builds up to the book's liberating conclusion, and Tony Ross's illustrations are full of his trademark humour and detail. RA 5+/IL 3-7

Cow

Malachy Doyle, illustrated by Angelo Rinaldi

Pocket Books £4.99 ISBN: 0 743 46215 7

If you or your child have ever wondered what it's like to be a cow then this is the book for you. If you haven't, buy it anyway just for the illustrations!

Malachy Doyle's gentle text is brought to life by breathtakingly beautiful pictures, which take the reader right into the field to experience a day in the life of a cow.

This is an immensely appealing book for children and adults of all ages, whether they are familiar with the countryside or not. RA 6+/IL 3-7

The Birdwatchers

Simon James

Walker Books £4.99 ISBN: 0 7445 9802 8

Grandad tells Jess that when he goes birdwatching amazing things happen: birds sometimes make drawings of him, and when he can't find them in his identification book, they point themselves out to him.

Jess sceptically accompanies Grandad to the woods – a favourite Simon James location – where she is amazed to discover … nothing. Gradually, however, with some help, she manages to see a great variety of birds, including dancing penguins who share her sandwich (or so she tells Grandad).

The bucolic illustrations that accompany Simon James's simple story are brought to life with exuberant splashes of watercolour. Jess is a cute little so-and-so, perfectly happy to spend time with her lovely Grandad. This sweet picture book is a touching evocation of a happy relationship. RA 6+/IL 3-7

Books for 5-8 Year-olds

These books are ideal for children who are just starting to read for themselves, or they can be read aloud by adults in order to help build the confidence of young readers. Bright and lively illustrations are still important for capturing the imagination, and the text should be bold and clear.

Children will eventually progress from reading each word separately, to putting them together to make a sentence, and then finally to understanding the story as a whole. The stories at the end of this section are longer, more demanding and more fulfilling for confident readers.

Tiny

Paul Rogers, illustrated by Korky Paul

Red Fox £5.99 ISBN: 0 09 940427 3

Tiny is a flea who lives on a dog called Cleopatra, who lives at 72 Hilltop Road in a town called Remembrance, on an island called Great Hope, on a planet called Earth.

When you're only as big as a flea, it's easy to feel insignificant, but one night Tiny looks up at the stars and realises that some of them are even smaller than he is. Suddenly, he doesn't feel quite so small after all.

This is an enjoyable way of looking at the world in perspective and understanding the importance of feeling happy with one's self. RA 5+/IL 3-6

Shine

Karen Langley, illustrated by Jonathan Langley

Frances Lincoln £5.99 ISBN: 0 7112 2116 2

Jimmy is given the part of the star in the school Christmas play, and practises 'shining' every day. His excitement and anxiety in the build-up to his appearance are contrasted with his busy dad's duties as the town electrician – will dad's last minute call-out to fix the Christmas lights stop him from seeing the play?

The central father-son relationship in this book is celebrated throughout in a manner both straightforward and sensitive and the illustrations glow with comfort and warmth. RA 5+/IL 3-7

Handa's Hen

Eileen Browne

Walker Books £4.99 ISBN: 0 7445 9815 X

Handa has lost Mondi, her black hen, and asks for help to find her. Handa and her friend Akeyo look everywhere for the hen but what they find instead is a cavalcade of unusual and exotic African animals, such as lizards, sunbirds, bullfrogs, spoonbills and many others.

This is a colourful and entertaining story about numbers, with a wonderful surprise at the end. Ideal for bedtime reading or for storytime sessions. RA 5+/IL 3-7

Mole and the Baby Bird

Marjorie Newman,
illustrated by Patrick Benson
Bloomsbury Children's Books £5.99
ISBN: 0 7475 6119 2

In this heartbreaking gem of a story, Mole finds a baby bird and takes it home. His dad warns him that baby birds usually die, but Mole, with his mum's help, nurses his pet to health. When he decides to build it a cage, however, Grandad's wisdom – and a walk in the wild wind – show Mole what he must really do.

This masterly picture book combines a beautifully restrained, simple text with wonderfully expressive illustrations to show how hard it can be to let go of a well-loved friend. RA 5+/IL 3-7

Lost on the Beach

Ian Beck
Scholastic Children's Books £5.99 ISBN: 0 439 98218 9

Teddy is left alone on the beach while Lily and Mum go to buy an ice cream. An inquisitive puppy comes along, drags Teddy along the beach and abandons him. He has fun splashing around in rock pools for a while, but then the tide starts coming in. With a little help from a passing seagull, and several ingenious ideas of his own, Teddy eventually makes it safely back to the beach.

This enjoyable story is accompanied by Ian Beck's atmospheric and charmingly old-fashioned illustrations. RA 6+/IL 3-7

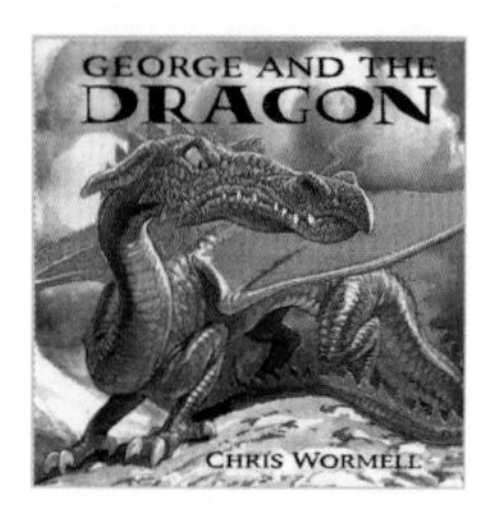

George and the Dragon

Chris Wormell
Red Fox £5.99 ISBN: 0 09 941766 9

The dragon in this tale is a fire-breathing beast who can fly higher than the clouds and faster than the birds, and knock down castles with his tail, but there's one thing that makes him cower in fear. When this terrifying creature moves in next door, the dragon soon forgets about the beautiful maiden he's brought back for lunch, and flees. This is good news for the maiden, and the dragon's new neighbour, George the mouse, who is soon relocated to a luxury hole in the castle wall.

This is a witty modernisation of a popular legend. RA 5+/IL 3-7

Helpful Henry

Ruth Brown

Andersen Press £4.99 ISBN: 1 84270 242 4

Ruth Brown perfectly depicts the daily activities of Henry, a pre-school boy who is desperate to help his mum with the household chores. He polishes the bathroom floor (with his dad's facecloth!), does the washing (including the cat!) and helps his dad with the painting – with predictable consequences! However, it is only when he starts school that Henry finds that his helping hand is truly appreciated.

The expressive artwork is full of bright colours that serve to strengthen and emphasise the spirit of this rhyming tale. RA 6+/IL 3-7

Green Light for the Little Red Train

Benedict Blathwayt

Red Fox £4.99 ISBN: 0 09 926502 8

The Little Red Train is following a new route; the guard tells Duffy the Driver to 'keep going as long as the lights are green.' Duffy obeys his orders but does not realise that he has taken the train through the Channel Tunnel. The Little Red Train travels through France, Spain, and Italy before eventually stopping at a red light and returning home, via a cross-Channel ferry.

The pictures in this book contain a wealth of detail to be pored over for hours. RA 6+/IL 3-7

Little Rabbit Lost

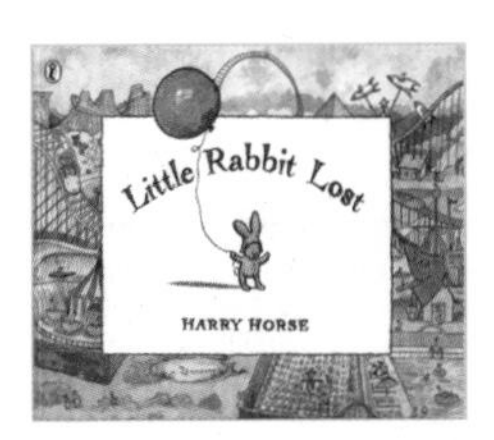

Harry Horse

Puffin £4.99 ISBN: 0 140 56851 4

On his birthday, Little Rabbit is given a huge red balloon and tickets to the Rabbit World theme park. Best of all though, he now thinks of himself as a 'big' rabbit.

At Rabbit World the family has a wonderful time, but when Little Rabbit is not allowed on some rides because he is too small, he gets fed up, wanders off and gets lost. Alone and confused, Little Rabbit realises he's not as big as he thought he was.

This tale is really brought to life by the bright and fascinatingly-detailed illustrations, which have a superb 'rabbitty' feel. RA 6+/IL 3-7

What Do You Remember?

Paul Stewart, illustrated by Chris Riddell

Andersen Press £4.99 ISBN: 1 84270 229 7

When Rabbit and Hedgehog play the 'remembering game', they have different memories of the same events. Hedgehog insists that Rabbit's memories are wrong, and Rabbit becomes agitated with his bossy friend. The pair begin to argue, but when Hedgehog forgets about the wobbly stepping stone halfway across the river and plunges into the water, Rabbit hauls him out and their friendship is restored.

The close relationship between these two delightful characters is heart-warming, though never overly sentimental. Chris Riddell's gentle illustrations are touched with humour and perfectly capture the spirit of the tale. RA 6+/IL 3-7

The Flyaway Alphabet

Mary Murphy

Egmont £4.99 ISBN: 1 4052 0535 0

When the alphabet keeper decides to clean a cage containing the letters of the alphabet, she does not expect them to fly around the room. She tries desperately to catch the letters, but they do not obey her: the letter 'p' flips upside down, turning the 'park' into 'bark', the 'h' flies down and turns a 'bus' into a 'bush' and so on.

This is an ingenious and amusing picture book that will encourage young readers to play and experiment with letters and words. RA 5+/IL 4-7

Penguin Post

Debi Gliori

Picture Corgi £5.99 ISBN: 0 552 54695 X

Milo is the youngest in a long line of Penguin Post penguins. But not for long. When Milo's mum goes out to look for food, leaving her unhatched egg with Milo's dad, Milo offers to deliver the mail. He travels all over The Pole delivering packages of all shapes and sizes, until there is only one item left in his sack. This turns out to be the egg Dad is supposed to be looking after, and it's about to hatch!

This beautifully-written tale helps to explain the importance of having responsibility, and the feelings associated with expecting a new baby. RA 6+/IL 4-7

Smog the City Dog

Adria Meserve

Red Fox £4.99 ISBN: 0 09 943227 7

Smog is a hungry stray dog who snatches a shopping bag full of food and runs off to find a place to eat the contents. However, there are other hungry animals in the city and Smog is soon being followed by Fox, Cat, Squirrel, Mouse and Hedgehog. Smog runs again and loses all the food in the canal. Fortunately, Mouse comes up with a plan and soon the food is retrieved and shared by all the friends.

This endearing book is a simple celebration of the importance of teamwork, friendship and food. RA 6+/IL 4-7

Dirty Bertie

David Roberts

Little Tiger Press £4.99 ISBN: 1 85430 820 3

Bertie has some very dirty habits. He eats sweets he finds on the pavement, picks his nose, licks the dog, and even pees in the garden! However, he soon learns that his unhygienic practices can have unpleasant consequences, and endeavours to give them all up. Well… almost all of them!

This fun picture book perfectly captures the not-so-nice side of a typical little boy. Children will laugh out loud at the hilarious illustrations and will love joining in with the repetitive chorus of 'No, Bertie! That's dirty, Bertie!' RA 5+/IL 4-7

The Smartest Giant in Town

Julia Donaldson, illustrated by Axel Scheffler

Macmillan Children's Books £5.99 ISBN: 0 333 963962

George is the scruffiest giant in town, so he buys a new outfit to smarten himself up. On the way home, however, he meets others who are in greater need of his clothes than he is, so he gradually gives away each new item of clothing. His tie becomes a scarf for a giraffe and his shoe makes an ideal home for a family of mice. When he arrives home, the animals he has helped are all waiting for him with a thank you present.

The repetitive text in this lovely tale is great to read aloud and the colourful illustrations are full of amusing details. RA 5+/IL 4-7

Someone Bigger

Jonathan Emmett, illustrated by Adrian Reynolds

Oxford University Press £4.99 ISBN: 0 19 272559 9

Sam and Dad make a kite and take it out to fly on a windy day. Sam is not allowed to hold the kite string because this job requires 'someone bigger' but then the wind blows so hard that Dad is lifted up into the sky. From then on everyone joins in trying to pull the kite down with amusing results!

With its rhyming text and repetition, this is a delightful story about the frustrations of being a small child. RA 6+/IL 4-7

Muncha! Muncha! Muncha!

Candace Fleming, illustrated by G. Brian Karas

Pocket Books £4.99 ISBN: 0 743 46204 1

Mr McGreely decides to grow vegetables in his garden but he hasn't reckoned on competition from three hungry bunnies! Each morning he builds a variety of devices to keep them out and each night, much to his increasing annoyance, they thwart his efforts and find a way in.

Children will love joining in with all the sound effects in this enchanting and funny book. RA 6+/IL 4-7

Rory and His Great Idea

Andrew Wolffe, illustrated by Tom Cole

Keppel Publishing £4.99 ISBN: 0 9534949 5 0

The hot weather is suffocating Sandy Bay, but Rory and his dog are cooling down on the beach. When Captain Campbell tells them that something strange is drifting towards the bay, Rory promises to keep an eye on things, but then he feels thirsty and finds he has nothing to drink.

He goes to the café, but it has run out of ice cream and the cold drinks machines are out of order. When Rory realises that the object in the bay is a large iceberg, he comes up with a great idea.

This is a simple, appealing book for younger readers. RA 6+/IL 4-7

Bertie Was a Watchdog

Rick Walton, illustrated by Arthur Robins

Walker Books £4.99 ISBN: 0 7445 8018 8

Bertie is the smallest watchdog ever: he's about the size of a watch, in fact. When a horrible robber comes calling, Bertie proves that, actually, it can be better to be small and clever rather than big and stupid...

Young children will love the humour, and the satisfying justice of the book's ending. Few readers of any age will be able to resist laughing out loud at Arthur Robins's hilarious illustrations, which perfectly match the amusing text. RA 6+/IL 4-7

The Very Kind Rich Lady and Her One Hundred Dogs

Chinlun Lee

Walker Books £5.99 ISBN: 0 7445 8933 9

If you like dogs as much as the very kind rich lady does, this is the book for you. Each of her one hundred dogs has a name, a plate and at least one flea. They are different shapes, sizes and colours, and they are all very happy (even Bingo, who is always late).

Children will love counting the dogs and memorising their names. With its deceptively naïve and comical illustrations, this is a book that gets funnier with every reading. RA 6+/IL 4-7

Underwater Farmyard

Carol Ann Duffy, illustrated by Joel Stewart

Macmillan Children's Books £4.99 ISBN: 0 333 96064 5

The mermaid reads the calves
a bedtime fable
While the horse and the goat
pillow-fight in the stable.

Down in the underwater farmyard, things look slightly different: webbed-feet sheep graze on salty seaweed, herds of seacows float and moo, water pigs snuffle out truffles for tea and fish-eyed goats nuzzle anchors in the sea.

Poet Carol Ann Duffy's warm and slightly surreal rhyming text is perfectly complemented by Joel Stewart's endearing and wonderfully atmospheric illustrations in this dreamy, delightful bedtime read. RA 6+/IL 4-7

The Wrong Overcoat

Hiawyn Oram, illustrated by Mark Birchall

Andersen Press £4.99 ISBN: 1 84270 211 4

Poor Chimp has been given a new purple overcoat and he's very unhappy about it: it's far too long, he doesn't like the colour, the collar scratches and the sleeves are so tight he can't even bowl properly! An encounter with a kaftan-clad kangaroo produces the perfect solution and the resourceful Chimp is able to choose his own new coat.

This is a vibrant and witty rendering of the familiar tussle over choosing clothes, and children will appreciate the conclusion that individuality sometimes needs free rein – no matter how garish the result! RA 6+/IL 4-7

All for One

Jill Murphy

Walker Books £4.99 ISBN: 0 7445 9489 8

Marlon wants to play with Basher, Boomps-a-daisy and Alligatina – but they don't seem all that keen on playing with him. Marlon's mum and gran help him put together some great costumes to fit in with the others' games, but by the time he's ready, they've always moved on to something else. In the end, though, Marlon thinks of something so splendid to do that it's the others' turn to ask him if they can play.

This warm and cleverly-observed book will appeal to anyone who's ever felt left out of things, and Jill Murphy's detailed and tactile pictures are wonderfully absorbing. RA 6+/IL 4-7

Egg Drop

Mini Grey

Red Fox £5.99 ISBN: 0 09 943203 X

Egg has attitude. It has a burning ambition to fly and won't be told that it can't. It is very young and knows next to nothing. If only it had waited! As it throws itself from the top of a tower, it thinks it is flying, convinced it has cracked it. The ground comes up very fast and things get messy.

This wise and humorous story, accompanied by stylish and wickedly amusing illustrations will appeal to children and parents alike. Mini Grey has produced the first rebel egg! RA 6+/IL 4-7

Slow Loris

Alexis Deacon

Red Fox £5.99 ISBN: 0 09 941426 0

Slow Loris lives up to his name: he is so slow that the visitors to the zoo – and the other animals – think he's boring. However, appearances can be deceptive and when he wants to be, Slow Loris can be incredibly fast and really rather wild!

Alexis Deacon's soft brown-grey palette is enlivened by brighter spashes of colour, to emphasise the text, and the pictures contain enough detail for children to enjoy exploring them. This is a beautifully illustrated and amusing picture book, full of contrasts and gentle humour. RA 6+/IL 4-7

Big Foot

M. P. Robertson

Frances Lincoln £5.99 ISBN: 0 7112 2068 9

One 'fat moon night' a little girl plays a tune to the trees and a sad lonely song comes back in reply. Climbing down from her window she discovers huge footprints in the snow and follows them into a dark wood. Out of the darkness comes Big Foot, his gentle eyes shining with kindness. They play together in the snow, but when her hairy companion builds a snow Big Foot, the little girl is dismayed to see his icicle tears.

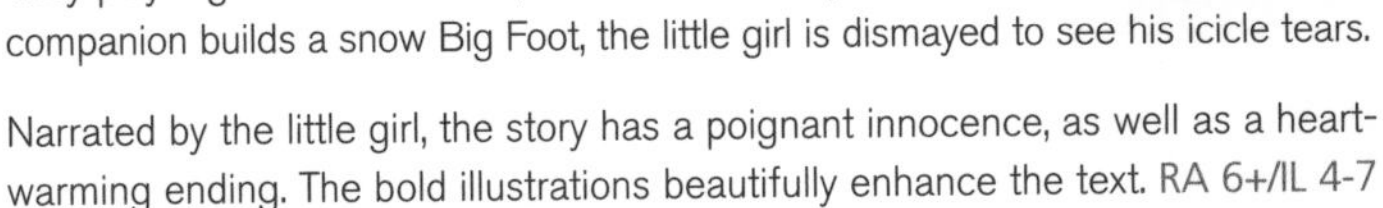

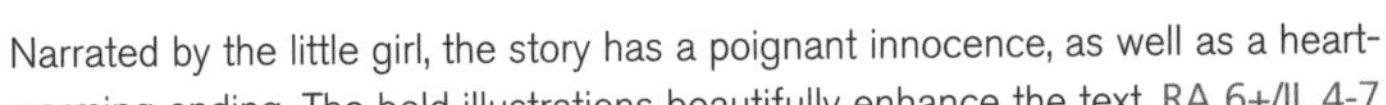

Narrated by the little girl, the story has a poignant innocence, as well as a heart-warming ending. The bold illustrations beautifully enhance the text. RA 6+/IL 4-7

I'm Not Invited?

Diana Cain Bluthenthal

Pocket Books £4.99 ISBN: 0 743 46813 9

When Minnie overhears that there is a party at her friend Charles's house on Saturday, she waits all week for an invitation; instead, she gets a note from him telling her he has named a mealworm after her! By the day of the party, she accepts that she has been overlooked and goes to play football instead. To her surprise, she finds that Charles, in a bid to escape his sister's party, is there too!

This touching book explores issues of friendship and, briefly, bullying. RA 6+/IL 4-8

The Wolf Who Cried Boy

Bob Hartman, illustrated by Tim Raglin

Lion Publishing £4.99 ISBN: 0 7459 4831 6

Little Wolf, tired of eating 'Lamburgers', dreams of delicious 'boy dishes', such as 'Baked Boy-tato'. Father Wolf says that if his son ever finds a boy in the woods, he will catch and cook him. In order to avoid eating his food, Little Wolf cries 'boy' every time dinner is served. Eventually, his parents get wise to his scheme and ignore his desperate cries of 'boy' when a scout troop goes by.

This is a hilarious reworking of Aesop's fable *The Boy Who Cried Wolf*, full of entertaining and expressive illustrations. RA 6+/IL 4-8

The Spider and the Fly

Mary Howitt, illustrated by Tony DiTerlizzi

Pocket Books £5.99 ISBN: 0 743 47817 7

This cautionary tale is based on a poem from 1829 by Mary Howitt, which begins: '"Will you walk into my parlour?" said the Spider to the Fly.' The fly, dressed in 1920s attire, comes to a sticky end when she is enticed into the spider's web by his flattering words.

The beautiful black-and-white illustrations are reminiscent of early twentieth-century silent films and there are plenty of humorous – and macabre – details on each page. RA 6+/IL 5-8

You've Got Dragons

Kathryn Cave, illustrated by Nick Maland

Hodder Children's Books £4.99 ISBN: 0 340 85159 7

Everybody has dragons! And Nick Maland's superb illustrations breathe new life into them. Precise and delicate cross hatched drawings, which borrow something from the world of animation, and a largely pastel palette prevent the dragons from being too scary and the details (such as a dragon banging a gong to wake Ben up in the morning or reclining on his plate at lunchtime) are hugely enjoyable.

This is a humorous, whimsical approach to a serious topic, with an important positive message at its heart. RA 6+/IL 5-8

The Four Franks

Sue Mayfield, illustrated by Garry Parsons

Egmont (Series: Blue Bananas) £3.99 ISBN: 1 4052 0674 8

To celebrate his sixth birthday Frank the fourth (he is named after his dad, grandpa and great-grandpa, who all live with him) is given a splendid sailing ship, made by his great-grandpa to look just like the one he went to sea in many years ago, and handed down through the generations.

But on her maiden voyage Frank's ship is swept away by the strong, swirling currents and he is too ashamed to tell anyone the truth. Then, during a walk on the beach the ship is recovered and all four Franks help to bring it back to its best.

This touching tale is another colourful *Blue Bananas* title for early readers, with related activities in the back. RA 6+/IL 5-8

Stan and the Crafty Cats

Scoular Anderson

A & C Black (Series: Rockets) £4.99 ISBN: 0 7136 6139 9

This is the fourth book in Scoular Anderson's series about the lovable, madcap Stan the Dog. Stan's normal routine consists mainly of eating and snoozing – the things he likes best – but this comfortable routine is interrupted by the arrival of some unwelcome guests: his family's former neighbour with her two prized cats, Clifford and Clementine!

Suddenly, snoozing becomes impossible, mealtimes turn into wartime and even walks are disastrous – Stan cannot wait until they all go home. But when first his new collar and then his new companions go missing, Stan must go to the rescue.
RA 6+/IL 5-8

The Colour of Home

Mary Hoffman, illustrated by Karin Littlewood

Frances Lincoln £5.99 ISBN: 0 7112 1991 5

On Hassan's first day at school he paints a colourful picture of his home and family in Somalia, but then adds soldiers, flames and bullets. A Somali translator helps him to explain that the painting shows his feelings about the death of his uncle, and his family's flight from Mogadishu to dreary England. But Hassan's next painting is full of colour, reflecting the hope and interest he begins to see in his new life in Britain.

This is an affecting yet ultimately optimistic tale, brought to life by expressive watercolour illustrations. RA 7+/IL 5-9

The Adventures of a Nose

Viviane Schwarz, illustrated by Joel Stewart

Walker Books £4.99 ISBN: 0 7445 9464 2

The Nose knows that there must be somewhere in the world where he can be happy, a place where he can fit in and stick out. Thus begins his frustrating search.

Joel Stewart's intriguing pictures reveal the Nose at the centre of a face wherever he travels, but the Nose can't see this, of course. Finally, he explains his worries to a doctor, who tells him what the reader already knows: that the whole world fits perfectly around HIM!

This is a masterly visual joke, and a gentle, surreal fable about finding your own place in the world. RA 6+/IL 6-9

The Nutcracker

Berlie Doherty, illustrated by Ian Beck

Picture Corgi £5.99 ISBN: 0 552 54834 0

On Christmas Eve young Clara is given a nutcracker by her Godfather, but little suspects the night of magic and romance that lies ahead.

Berlie Doherty's lyrical, delightfully old-fashioned prose is perfectly complemented by Ian Beck's charming illustrations. His attention to detail is superb, and the slightly soft focus invokes an atmosphere of intimacy. Enchanting! RA 7+/IL 5-8

Mrs McCool and the Giant Cúchulainn: An Irish Tale

Jessica Souhami

Frances Lincoln £5.99 ISBN: 0 7112 1823 4

This retelling of the story of the encounter between two of the greatest folk heroes of Celtic legend – the Giant Cúchulainn and his last remaining unconquered foe, Finn McCool – is a timeless tale of brain versus brawn.

The text is simply laid out in an uncluttered style, enhancing the impact of the lively, colourful illustrations. Jessica Souhami (an illustrator, puppeteer and former textile designer) draws on her knowledge of textiles and the large, vividly-coloured, paper cut-out figures, endowed with the characteristics and pronounced movements of puppets, really bring this tale alive. RA 7+/IL 5-8

Who's Afraid of the Big Bad Book?

Lauren Child

Hodder Children's Books £6.99 ISBN: 0 340 80555 2

Lauren Child uses a classic fairy-tale formula for this ingenious and original tale. Herb is drawn into a book of fairy tales where he visits many magic places and meets several well-known characters. But he constantly gets into trouble and spends most of his time trying to escape from these dangerous situations.

Inter-textual narrative has been used in countless children's books, but Lauren Child's quirky, hilarious collage illustrations, which work superbly well with the theme and style of the book, are what make this picture book special. RA 6+/IL 6-9

Larkspur and the Grand March

Mary Arrigan, illustrated by Debbie Boon

Egmont (Series: Red Bananas) £3.99 ISBN: 1 4052 0592 X

Davy loves music and his Aunt Becky loves opera. When *Aida* comes to the Royal Opera House they decide to go along and listen – from outside, as they can't afford tickets.

On the way, they encounter Larkspur, a very cultured lion, at the local zoo. Larkspur adores opera, so he joins them too, causing much consternation among the passers by. At the opera house Larkspur's enthusiasm is misinterpreted by the theatre-goers until the star, Signor Singalotti, comes up with a cunning plan. RA 7+/IL 6-9

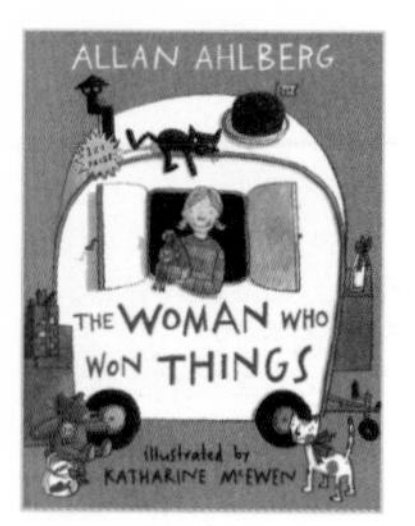

The Woman Who Won Things

Allan Ahlberg, illustrated by Katharine McEwen

Walker Books £5.99 ISBN: 0 7445 9496 0

The Gaskitts are an ordinary, slightly disorganised family, whose everyday life is enlivened by extraordinary events. When Mrs Gaskitt hits a winning streak, receiving prizes large and small, she begins to long for her old, less lucky, life. Her children meanwhile solve the mystery of their unusual supply teacher and the disappearing items.

This well-written, funny and exciting book for early readers is enhanced by Katharine McEwen's colourful, animated and informative pictures. RA 7+/IL 6-9

Queen Munch and Queen Nibble

Carol Ann Duffy, illustrated by Lydia Monks

Macmillan Children's Books £6.99 ISBN: 0 333 96066 1

This tale of two very different queens is huge fun. Queen Munch is big and loud and colourful. She loves eating and, every Saturday morning, her people gather to watch the public Munching of the Breakfast.

In contrast, Queen Nibble is tall and slender and pale as a stick of celery. She spends most of her time alone, making jewellery from raindrops. But when Queen Munch invites her to stay, Queen Nibble has no choice but to go – and both queens find out how being different can form the basis for a great friendship.

Beautifully complemented by vibrant illustrations. RA 7+/IL 6-9

The Countess's Calamity

Sally Gardner

Bloomsbury Children's Books £4.99 ISBN: 0 7475 5940 6

When a box containing five dolls from the land of Lounge is left under a park bench, the dolls are discovered and befriended by a pair of mice who do their best to keep them safe. Unfortunately, one doll, the Countess, who is proud and snobbish, won't co-operate and creates many difficulties for the others, as well as running into great personal danger, before she learns her lesson.

This is a touching and enjoyable story, about friendship and tolerance, which is ideal for reading aloud. RA 7+/IL 6-9

Judy Moody Predicts the Future

Megan McDonald, illustrated by Peter Reynolds

Walker Books £4.99 ISBN: 0 7445 8343 8

Judy Moody finds a 'mood ring' inside a box of cereal: it has an oogley centre that changes colour according to the wearer's mood. When Mr Todd, one of her teachers, confiscates the ring, it turns red – the colour of love – convincing Judy that she can predict the future. She becomes determined to prove that Mr Todd is in love with visiting writer Ms Tater.

Hugely entertaining from start to finish and perfectly complemented by black-and-white drawings, this book will capture the attention and imagination of the most reluctant reader. RA 7+/IL 6-9

The Four Ugly Cats in Apartment 3D

Marilyn Sachs, illustrated by Rosanne Litzinger

Simon & Schuster Children's Books £4.99
ISBN: 0 689 83728 3

One day Lily forgets her front door key. When unfriendly Mr Freeman grudgingly allows her to wait in his apartment, and introduces her to his four cats, Lily discovers an unsuspected, caring side to his nature. When he dies soon afterwards, she has only three days to find each cranky cat a new home.

Lily's boundless optimism, creative mind and determination transform her neighbours into a neighbourhood. Expressive charcoal sketches give character to this deceptively simple, urban fable about not accepting people – or cats! – at face value. RA 7+/IL 6-9

The Thief, the Fool and the Big Fat King

Terry Deary, illustrated by Helen Flook

A & C Black (Series: Tudor Tales) £4.99 ISBN: 0 7136 6434 7

Aided by Helen Flook's comic illustrations and told with the same gusto and zest for detail that have made his *Horrible Histories* such a success, Terry Deary spins another historical tale in his own inimitable style.

Set during the reign of Henry VIII, the story centres on a boy called James as he and his parents struggle to make a living as entertainers. When their takings are snatched by a young female cutpurse, Will Somers, the King's fool, offers them a chance to redeem their fortunes by performing before the 'Big Fat King' himself – that is until Henry turns out to be the biggest cheat of all! RA 7+/IL 6-10

The Amazing Adventures of Girl Wonder

Malorie Blackman, illustrated by Lis Toft

Barn Owl Books £3.99 ISBN: 1 903015 27 8

This compilation of *Girl Wonder* stories, selected (by the author) from two previous books, is centred on the often misguided, but irrepressibly good-humoured, adventures of Girl Wonder Maxine and her compliant twin brothers Edward and Antony.

These warm tales of a single-parent Afro-Caribbean family, related with Malorie Blackman's usual skill and based on everyday incidents of family life, are both fun and easy to read. Mum, though kind and patient (as well as unfailingly good-natured), also bucks the usual stereotype by displaying accomplished technical skills (such as mending the car), while young readers will readily identify with the sparky Maxine. RA 7+/IL 6-9

Princess Mirror-Belle

Julia Donaldson, illustrated by Lydia Monks

Macmillan Children's Books £3.99 ISBN: 0 330 41530 1

Ellen, off school with chicken pox, gets a big surprise one day while examining her spots in the mirror: her reflection starts talking back to her, and even comes out of the mirror! She is Princess Mirror-Belle, a magical princess from a faraway land, and she leads Ellen into all sorts of trouble.

Princess Mirror-Belle, written in short, easy-to-manage chapters, is ideal for children who are just starting to read alone. RA 7+/IL 6-9

Blobheads

Paul Stewart, illustrated by Chris Riddell

Macmillan Children's Books £4.99 ISBN: 0 330 41353 8

Ever wondered what might rise out of the toilet when you lift the lid? In Billy Barnes's case it's the Blobheads, three incompetent aliens who are looking for the High Emperor of the Universe in order to save him from the evil Followers of Sandra. Unfortunately, they wrongly identify Billy's baby brother as the Emperor, and cause mayhem in their efforts to protect him.

Readers will identify with the Blobheads' shortcomings and Billy's realisation that he actually loves his annoying brother. A comically outrageous but thought-provoking collection of four short novels in one volume, ideal for newly fluent readers.
RA 8+/IL 6-10

Books for 9-12 Year-olds

Once children have mastered the art of reading for themselves, it is important to build their confidence and retain their interest by keeping them supplied with a diverse selection of good fiction.

This section includes titles that will challenge and surprise the reader right up to the final page. An intriguing variety of subjects encourages children to turn their imaginations to more demanding stories.

The Nightingale

Hans Christian Andersen, retold by Stephen Mitchell, illustrated by Bagram Ibatoulline

Walker Books £6.99 ISBN: 0 7445 9840 0

The Emperor of China lives in a porcelain palace set in sumptuous gardens where the rarest flowers are tied with tinkling silver bells. Visitors from around the world come and exclaim in wonder, but loveliest of all, they say, is the song of the nightingale that sings in the trees edging the seashore.

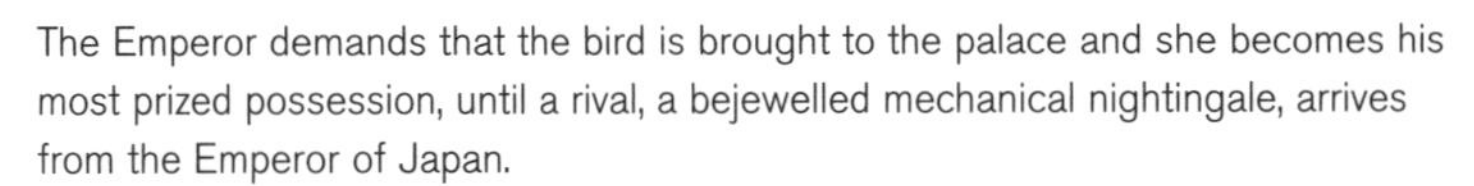

The Emperor demands that the bird is brought to the palace and she becomes his most prized possession, until a rival, a bejewelled mechanical nightingale, arrives from the Emperor of Japan.

This sensitive retelling brings the story into focus for today's readers and Bagram Ibatoulline's inspired illustrations are a joy. RA 8+/IL 6-11

The Boy with the Magic Numbers

Sally Gardner

Dolphin £3.99 ISBN: 1 84255 088 8

Billy Pickles is confused and upset when his Dad leaves for New York without saying goodbye, but is fascinated by a strange money-box that has been left behind for him.

When he eventually visits his father and his Italian grandmother in the United States, he takes the money-box with him. This mysteriously starts to recite seemingly random numbers, which leads Billy and his family into all sorts of scrapes and adventures, including safe-cracking and kidnapping.

This is a fun-packed and fast-paced fantasy adventure. RA 8+/IL 6-11

Memorial

Gary Crew, illustrated by Shaun Tan

Lothian £4.99 ISBN: 0 7344 0545 6

'My great-grandpa says they planted the tree on the day he came home from the war.' This was 1918 but the tree is a memorial to all the conflicts of the twentieth-century and each page contains poignant symbols of war, summoned up by evocative and highly original illustrations.

Combining drawing, painting, textiles, collage and ephemera Shaun Tan creates delicately resonant images to echo the text: the fractured, peeling surface of plaster, ragged-edged hessian, bloodied bandages, sepia-coloured papers and faded postmarks, interspersed with life-affirming images of seeds, flowers, leaves and of course, the tree itself, all reinforce the importance of memories, especially shared ones. RA 7+/IL 7-12

Maisie Morris and the Awful Arkwrights

Joanna Nadin, illustrated by Arthur Robins

Walker Books £4.99 ISBN: 0 7445 9091 4

Withering Heights Retirement Home is the unlikely residence of our heroine Maisie Morris. She shares it with her mother (its downtrodden housekeeper), the unfortunate but colourful residents, and its ghastly owners, the Arkwrights.

The dastardly Arkwrights' days are numbered when a new guest, Mr Cummerbund, arrives accompanied by Monkey Onassis (a small international jewel thief), a gigantic flying four-poster bed, his own peculiar brand of magic, and an ingenious plan for revenge.

Joanna Nadin's flamboyant prose bounds along, disguising a shrewd satire on contemporary attitudes to age in a light-hearted tale of wish-fulfilment. RA 8+/IL 7-10

The Quigleys

Simon Mason, illustrated by Helen Stephens

Corgi Yearling £4.99 ISBN: 0 440 86499 2

Each of these four short stories focuses on a different member of the Quigley family. Dad is shown in an unheroic light when he loses one of the neighbour's children he is supposed to be babysitting; Lucy gets her own way and becomes a bridesmaid dressed as a bee; Mum shows how family love can turn the worst birthday into the best birthday ever; and Will's loyalty to a friend is rewarded, instead of punished as he fears.

This funny collection gives young readers an agreeable sense of the absurdities of everyday life. RA 8+/IL 8-11

Spook School

Sue Purkiss, illustrated by Lynne Chapman

A & C Black £4.99 ISBN: 0 7136 6292 1

Spooker Batt is a ghost boy who attends the Anne Boleyn Secondary School. The Practical Haunting exam is rapidly approaching and the pupils must put into practice what they have learned so far. Spooker, who is not good at scaring people, is initially disappointed with his haunting assignment – an ordinary house in Somerset – but on his arrival he meets Ben Roper, a boy his own age, and discovers a real purpose to his visit.

This is an amusing tale with strongly-drawn characters. RA 8+/IL 8-11

Captain Underpants and the Big, Bad Battle of the Bionic Booger Boy

Part 1: The Night of the Nasty Nostril Nuggets

Dav Pilkey

Scholastic Children's Books £4.99 ISBN: 0 439 97736 3

George, Harold and Captain Underpants step in to save the day. Firstly, when 'brainiac' Melvin Sneedley tries to transform himself into a Bionic-Powered Superboy, and later, when three humongous robotic booger chunks come to life.

Although the finer points of the *Captain Underpants* books may escape adults, Year 7 and 8 boys, who exult in the toilet humour – the more disgusting, the better – will read their copies ragged. The illustrations – part cartoon, part comic strip – are also very effective. RA 8+/IL 8-11

Starring Sammie

Helena Pielichaty, illustrated by Melanie Williamson
Oxford University Press (Series: After School Club) £3.99
ISBN: 0 19 275247 2

Zetland Avenue Primary School After School Club (ZAPS) not only organises exciting activities, but also allows Sammie a place where she can feel safe and relaxed away from the pressures of home and school life. When a fund-raising venture goes wrong and Mum spends the sponsor money on new boots, Sammie does something very foolish, which risks losing the trust and friendship she has only just established.

Part of a series of stories, this is an unpretentious tale, told in a familiar, chatty style, addressing issues which often worry or affect young children. RA 8+/IL 7-11

Meet the Weirds

Kaye Umansky, illustrated by Chris Mould
Barrington Stoke £4.99 ISBN: 1 84299 114 0

This is an amusing story about two very different neighbouring families. The Primm parents are horrified when the Weirds move in next door and forbid young Pinchton Primm from mixing with them. But the messy, untidy Weird children prove enticingly friendly and there are lots of surprises in store for Pinchton as he gets to know them.

This lively, entertaining tale, aimed at reluctant readers, is full of genuinely funny situations, enhanced by the excellent cartoons. RA 8+/IL 8-11

The Mum Hunt

Gwyneth Rees, illustrated by Chloë March
Macmillan Children's Books £4.99 ISBN: 0 330 41012 1

Esmie's mum died when she was born, so her dad has brought up both Esmie and her older brother Matthew on his own.

When Esmie is 11, she decides it's about time her dad got himself a new girlfriend and is convinced, after watching *The Sound of Music*, that her French au pair Juliette is the perfect choice. Juliette has other ideas, however, and together they place a lonely hearts ad in the newspaper, with unexpected results.

A funny, moving and unusual slant on single-parent families. RA 8+/IL 8-11

Horrendo's Curse

Anna Fienberg, illustrated by Kim Gamble

Allen & Unwin £4.99 ISBN: 1 86508 603 7

A spell was cast on Horrendo when he was a baby – he is unable to curse or swear, and must always be polite and kind. Consequently, he doesn't have any friends among his constantly-cursing fellow villagers. Not to mention that the village is plagued by a pirate ship that visits every year to steal away all the 12-year-old boys to spend two years aboard the ship; the few who survive their heartless treatment are later returned to the village.

But when Horrendo and his class-mates are kidnapped, he shows them that a good meal, teamwork and a few kind words can make a big difference, and leads them to a buried hoard of pirate treasure.

A heartwarming, swashbuckling adventure on the high seas, aimed at confident readers. RA 9+/IL 8-10

Granny Nothing

Catherine MacPhail, illustrated by Sarah Nayler

Scholastic Children's Books £4.99 ISBN: 0 439 98287 1

Granny Nothing arrives on the McAllisters' doorstep and turns everything upside down! Baby Thomas adores her, Stephanie and Ewen aren't too sure, but the adults are united in wishing her a long way away.

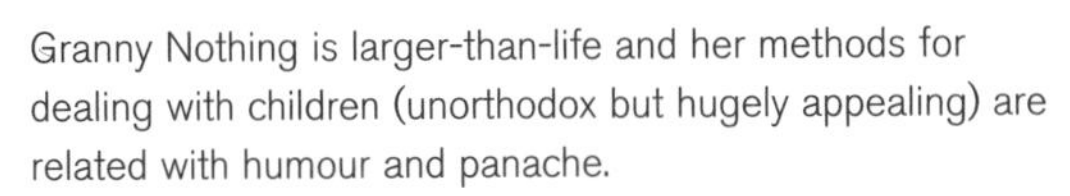
Granny Nothing is larger-than-life and her methods for dealing with children (unorthodox but hugely appealing) are related with humour and panache.

This is a refreshingly well-written book, where those who deserve it get their come-uppance and no bones about it. Granny Nothing, though often embarrassing and certainly eccentric, is the one who has the most insight and understanding of the children's problems. A warm and funny read for newly-confident readers.
RA 8+/IL 8-12

The Sleeping Sword

Michael Morpurgo, illustrated by Michael Foreman
Egmont £4.99 ISBN: 1 40 520492 3

This Arthurian tale, set in the Scilly Isles, is a story within a story. Ten-year-old Bun Bendle, blinded in a freak accident, falls into a huge hole in one of his father's fields. The hole is, in fact, an ancient tomb, and hidden within it he finds a remarkably well-preserved sword and shield. When Bun takes hold of the sword, an incredible power surges through him and changes his life forever.

Like Michael Morpurgo's other stories, this is a convincing and compelling tale that illustrates beautifully the value of friendship, family and positive thinking. RA 8+/IL 8-13

Sam Hawkins, Pirate Detective, and the Case of the Cut-Glass Cutlass

Ian Billings, illustrated by Sam Hearn
Macmillan Children's Books £4.99 ISBN: 0 330 41497 6

This over-the-top adventure finds Sam Hawkins, once the finest swashbuckler ever to sail the Seven Seas, turning 'pirate detective' to catch the thieves of the legendary cut-glass cutlass. Taking in a dancing octopus, the wickedest pirate in all Spain, and a whole bag of red herrings along the way, Sam's exploits are packed with fun and wildly inventive language.

Enhanced by atmospheric pictures, this hugely enjoyable book guarantees many chuckles and plenty of reading practice. RA 9+/IL 8-12

The Great Good Thing

Roderick Townley
Simon & Schuster £4.99 ISBN: 0 689 83714 3

Sylvie is bored with her life as a 12-year-old storybook princess – after all, she has been living it for the past 80 years. So one day she does a Forbidden Thing and looks at her Reader, a troubled young girl called Claire. Thus, Sylvie is able to enter into the new, exciting and dangerous world of Claire's dreams and memories.

But as Claire grows up and there are no more Readers, Sylvie's life, and those of all the storybook people she loves, comes under threat and she must do 'one great, good thing' to save them all. This is a lively, original, witty novel. RA 9+/IL 8-12

Everything on a Waffle

Polly Horvath

Scholastic Children's Books £4.99 ISBN: 0 439 98289 8

Primrose Squarp is 11 years old, lives in a fishing village in British Columbia, and refuses to accept everyone else's view that she is an orphan.

Although her parents never returned from a typhoon at sea, Primrose is convinced that one day they will. In the meantime she is cared for by several well-meaning, if unconventional, inhabitants. She learns to cook (and writes down her recipes for us) and goodnaturedly suffers a number of unfortunate accidents.

Funny, touching and more profound than at first it appears, this is justifiably a Newbery Honor Book. RA 9+/IL 8-12

Abraham Hannibal and the Raiders of the Sands

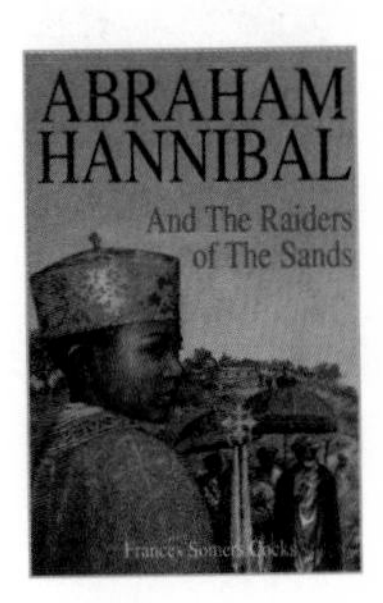

Frances Somers Cocks, illustrated by Eric Robson

Goldhawk Press £5.99 ISBN: 0 9544034 0 1

Set in eighteenth-century Ethiopia, this novel (based on a true story) concerns the son of a noble African lord who visits the royal city Gondar with his father. He is ordered by the Emperor to represent the youth of Ethiopia at the court of Louis XIV of France, but the voyage proves to be a dangerous one. Abraham is sold into slavery, then shipwrecked.

This well-researched novel highlights a little-known area of black history; its gripping narrative style, strong characterisation and convincing plot are complemented by full-page black-and-white drawings that provide a flavour of life in Africa during the eighteenth century. Look out for the sequel, *Abraham Hannibal and the Battle of the Throne.* RA 9+/IL 8-12

Molly Moon's Incredible Book of Hypnotism

Georgia Byng

Macmillan Children's Books £4.99 ISBN: 0 330 39985 3

Molly Moon is dreadfully unhappy at Hardwick House Orphanage. She has no self-confidence, is bullied, and feels unloved. When she discovers an ancient book about hypnotism, her dismal life changes drastically and she develops hypnotic powers, which bring her stardom in a Broadway show. However, an evil stranger is determined to use her powers for his own ends...

An entertaining novel, with an engaging plot and ingenious final twist. RA 9+/IL 8-13

Ruby Holler

Sharon Creech

Bloomsbury Children's Books £5.99 ISBN: 0 7475 6029 3

Dallas and Florida are the oldest children in the Boxton Creek Home. Disillusioned by the poor treatment they receive, they have low expectations of their latest placing with Tiller and Sairy Morey. However, Tiller and Sairy are an unusual couple who believe that children should have the freedom to make their own choices.

This is a life-affirming story of a group of seemingly mismatched people who find that being together gives their lives new purpose. *Ruby Holler* is a testament to the power of tolerance, determination, love, and optimism. RA 9+/IL 8-13

Ghost Writer

Julia Jarman

Scholastic Children's Books £4.99 ISBN: 0 439 97854 8

Frankie Ruggles DBNT (Dyslexic But Not Thick) has just moved to a new school. Not only does he have to cope with making new friends, explaining his dyslexia and being taught by the terrifying Miss Bulpit, he's also visited by the ghost of a Victorian boy. Frankie develops strategies to cope with his dyslexia, but ultimately, it's his new friends who help him out when he needs them most.

This spooky ghost story also gives an insight into the everyday difficulties faced by dyslexics. RA 9+/IL 8-13

Pure Dead Wicked

Debi Gliori

Corgi £4.99 ISBN: 0 552 54847 2

This is the second book about the Strega-Borgia family, their butler, nanny and pets. Their ancestral castle is leaking so badly that the family has to move into a local hotel while the roof is being repaired. Chaos ensues and there is plenty of humour, magic, action and suspense. Surrounded by fantasy and magic, the two children are recognisably real-life characters; the others tend to be caricatures but are very funny.

Debi Gliori has a wonderful imagination and has created some hilarious and exciting situations that will appeal to those who enjoy mayhem and lavatorial jokes. RA 9+/IL 8-13

The Chaos Clock

Gill Arbuthnot

Floris Books £4.99 ISBN: 0 86315 422 0

Two 11-year-old children, Kate and David, friends in contemporary Edinburgh, find themselves increasingly drawn to the local museum, particularly to the new exhibit, the Millennium clock, with its strange, carved little monkey figure.

Peculiar noises and dreams and their meetings with Kate's late grandma's old friend, John Flowerdew, soon draw them into the heart of a mystery, which has its roots in a distant battle between the Guardians of Time and the Lords of Chaos. Only the children can defeat Chaos, but to do so they must confront their own demons.

This time-slip novel is a great read: convincingly narrated with good characterisation, a plot full of mystery and suspense, and a palpable sense of history. RA 9+/IL 8-13

Flying with Icarus

Curdella Forbes

Walker Books £4.99 ISBN: 0 7445 9067 1

This collection contains seven stories about modern Caribbean life, tautly written in poetic and evocative language that captures both the carefree, sunny existence of the islands, and a deeper mystical experience.

Each tale addresses universal concerns (childhood unhappiness and uncertainties, bullies, social outcasts) but delivers reassurance and wisdom via situations specific to the Caribbean setting.

An unusual and compelling anthology, equally relevant to readers in Kingston, Jamaica, Kingston upon Hull and Kingston on Thames. RA 10+/IL 9-12

How to Train Your Dragon

Cressida Cowell

Hodder Children's Books £5.99 ISBN: 0 340 86068 5

This story of Vikings and dragons is an absolute joy! Hiccup is the son of the chief and as such is expected to be brave and fierce; unfortunately, he is more interested in natural history.

When a giant Seadragon attacks the island, intent on eating the inhabitants, the ferocious bravado of the other Vikings proves useless; instead, Hiccup is called upon to save the tribe by using brains rather than brawn.

Youngsters will love the sharp wit, dry humour and lavatorial humour of Cressida Cowell's story, which is decorated with black-and-white sketches of dragons and Vikings. RA 9+/IL 9-13

My Mum and the Hound from Hell

Meg Harper

Lion Publishing £4.99 ISBN: 0 7459 4799 9

In the third and final volume of the *My Mum* series, Kate has to contend with more embarrassing and difficult situations when her somewhat eccentric mother adopts the rather unruly dog of an emigrating neighbour, her best friend is banished to boarding school, and a gorgeous new boy arrives in her class.

This well-written and thoroughly amusing book about love, relationships and responsibilities is peopled by realistic characters and summons up lots of enjoyable teenage angst. RA 10+/IL 9-12

Broken

Penny Kendal

Andersen Press £5.99 ISBN: 1 84270 174 6

Rebecca and Jack don't even know they have an aunt until their mum goes into rehab to kick heroin and they are sent to their aunt's house in Southwold.

Dreading being taken into care, 13-year-old Rachel struggles to control her rebellious younger brother Jack, but when they are forbidden from entering one particular room, Jack just can't resist. Finding it full of china dolls and accidentally breaking one, they don't understand the force of their aunt's reaction until strange events are set in motion and Rebecca becomes convinced that she is being haunted.

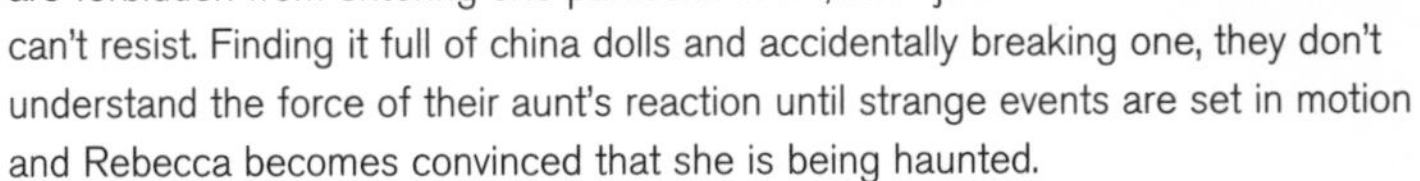

As the children struggle to cope with their mother's addiction and their estranged aunt, long-buried family secrets begin to surface. RA 9+/IL 9-13

At the Sign of the Sugared Plum

Mary Hooper

Bloomsbury Children's Books £5.99 ISBN: 0 7475 6124 9

It is 1665, and Hannah, the spirited heroine, is thrilled at the chance to visit London to help in her sister's sweetmeats shop, The Sugared Plum.

However, upon arrival she learns that plague is threatening to devastate the city and that behind the excitement of her new way of life (and first love) lurks the shadow of death. How will Hannah and her sister survive?

This lively and absorbing book convincingly conveys some of the sounds, smells and streetlife of seventeenth-century London. RA 10+/IL 9-13

Fish

L. S. Matthews

Hodder Children's Books £4.99 ISBN: 0 340 87403 1

Tiger's parents are aid workers in a war-torn country. As the conflict approaches their village, the family have to flee across the border without delay. A man with a donkey – the enigmatic Guide – accompanies them. Before they leave the village, Tiger catches a fish whose very survival somehow seems to be as important as their own.

This Fidler Award-winning novel is the story of the family's flight to safety and the dangers they encounter, including the threat of being taken hostage by desperate men in the mountains. RA 9+/IL 9-13

Lines in the Sand: New Writing about War and Peace

Compiled and edited by Mary Hoffman and Rhiannon Lassiter

Frances Lincoln £4.99 ISBN: 0 7112 2282 7

This anthology about war and peace contains poems, short stories and illustrations by 135 contributors from around the world. The result is a thought-provoking medley of messages fostering peace.

Although the book was compiled in response to the war in Iraq, a wide range of conflicts is considered, ranging from the Spanish Civil War to Croatia.

Inevitably, this book provides a political platform for many of the contributors, but the final and common message is clearly conveyed: No to war and Yes to peace! (Royalties and profits from the sale of this book are donated to UNICEF.) RA 9+/IL 9-13

Up on Cloud Nine

Anne Fine

Corgi £4.99 ISBN: 0 552 54840 5

Stol has fallen out of a top-floor window and lies, unmoving and unconscious, in a hospital bed. Keeping watch are his best friend Ian and Ian's mum. While he watches, waits and hopes for Stol to wake up, Ian decides to write about Stol's unusual life.

Normally, Stol is full of life, words and ideas. So why is it that sometimes he seems to be just teetering on the edge of this world? Why is he always having accidents and ending up in hospital? This is a witty, touching and memorable novel. RA 9+/IL 9-13

The Adventures of Jimmy Scar

Jeanne Willis

Andersen Press £4.99 ISBN: 1 84270 230 0

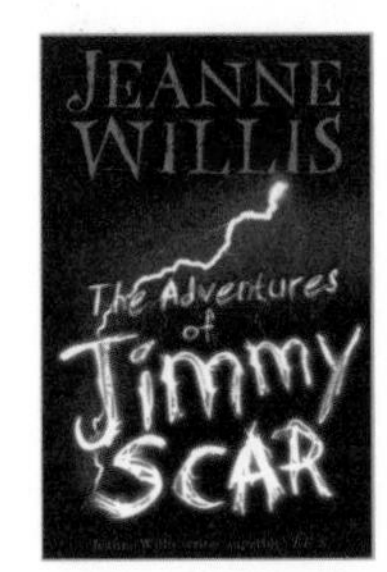

When Gemma's Dad is mistakenly arrested for burglary, she is forced to go on the run. She cuts her hair short and becomes 'Jimmy Scar', hiding out with an eccentric old woman who teaches her self sufficiency and survival skills. But who is the old woman and will Gemma be able to clear her father's name?

This is a tale of survival against the odds that raises thought-provoking social issues. RA 10+/IL 9-13

The Voyage of the Arctic Tern

Hugh Montgomery, illustrated by Nick Poullis

Walker Books £8.99 ISBN: 0 7445 9483 9

Montgomery's epic tale of seafaring, piracy, treachery and revenge is written, in the classical tradition, as a poem divided into three books.

The story follows Bruno – who is doomed, like the Flying Dutchman, to sail the oceans for eternity – as he seeks in our time to make reparations for the treachery he committed many centuries ago.

This fascinating and atmospherically illustrated book combines an excellent story with a most unusual format. RA 10+/IL 9+

The Rattletrap Trip

Rachel Anderson

Oxford University Press £4.99 ISBN: 0 19 271872 X

Sassy collects things nobody else wants. Luckily for Julia and her five siblings, this includes children. Sassy's latest impulsive idea is to set off into the wilderness in an old camper van, but living rough isn't as easy as it sounds and when their makeshift home catches fire, Julia expects her life to go back to normal.

Little does she know that a man on an aircraft will read about the fire in a newspaper, and decide that it's time to catch up with the daughter he left behind. This is a fascinating novel, told with warmth and humour. RA 10+/IL 9-13

A Wind from the Sea

Jennifer Morgan

Pont Books £4.99 ISBN: 1 84323 209 X

Liverpool, 1833. Patience's father has died, leaving her and her mother poverty stricken. She prepares to go to Wales to live on her Uncle Huw's farm for a time, but just before leaving, Patience befriends Xanthe, a frightened black girl who has made the terrifying sea journey from Antigua to escape a tyrannical slave master. It is decided that Xanthe will accompany Patience to Wales.

Set in the context of Wilberforce's anti-slavery Bill and the growing Abolitionist movement, Jennifer Morgan's book is an exciting tale of two girls facing up to the world as young women in difficult circumstances. RA 10+/IL 9-13

You Can't Kiss it Better

Diana Hendry

Red Fox £4.99 ISBN: 0 09 940347 1

Four foster children, each with their own problems, are cared for by the rather wonderful Megan. The house they inhabit overlooks a river, the nature of which seems to reflect the turbulent lives of the characters.

This wonderfully open and honest account of damaged children and of the resilience and humour that help them to survive, manages to combine serious subject matter with an entertaining plot. RA 10+/IL 9-13

The Wizard's Promise

Cliff McNish

Dolphin £4.99 ISBN: 1 85881 844 3

The final book in the *Doomspell* Trilogy follows Rachel and her brother Eric as they anticipate an attack on the magical children of Earth from the Griddas.

Fierce creatures bred by the High Witches on the planet Ool, the Griddas have turned against their creators to wreak death and havoc wherever they can. Yemi, the magical human child, doesn't understand the danger the Griddas represent, and it is up to Rachel and Eric to unlock their magical powers and save the Earth from destruction.

The power of Cliff McNish's imagination sweeps the reader headlong into the story and maintains the tension until its thrilling climax. An extraordinary, highly original fantasy novel. RA 10+/IL 9-13

Esperanza Rising

Pam Muñoz Ryan

The Chicken House £5.99 ISBN: 1 903 43498 X

Esperanza and her family are wealthy Mexicans who lose their land and money in the Great Depression of the 1930s. Forced to work for a meagre living in the vineyards and fruit fields of California, a life for which she is ill-prepared, Esperanza learns the true value of friendship and comes to appreciate what is really important in life.

This involving story about an interesting period in American history contains a universal message and is ultimately full of hope. RA 9+/IL 9-14

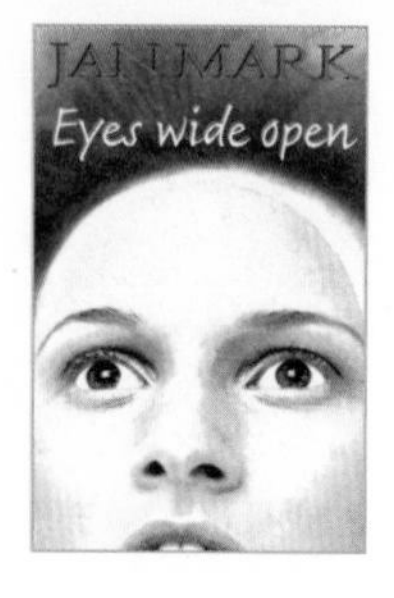

Eyes Wide Open

Jan Mark, illustrated by Scoular Anderson

A & C Black (Series: Black Cats) £4.99 ISBN: 0 7136 6717 6

In this collection of six highly readable stories Jan Mark takes a subtle journey into the secret self. The stories range from the comically humble beginnings of a self-made man in *Teeth*, to the knowledge that even parents have secret selves in *Dan, Dan the Scenery Man*, and finally, to the sort of understanding that comes with tolerance in *Eye Opener*.

This notion of knowledge, about the self and others, is the thread that unites these understated tales in a witty and stimulating read. RA 8+/IL 10-14

Bindi Babes

Narinder Dhami

Corgi Yearling £4.99 ISBN: 0 440 86512 3

The Bindi sisters seem to be coping very well following the death of their mother. They are popular at school and manage the housekeeping; their father buys them anything they want.

When their aunt comes over from India to look after them they resent the intrusion and resolve to get rid of her. This, however, proves to be difficult, and they begin to realise that in fact their lives are not so perfect.

Although these are serious themes, Narinder Dhami has a light touch, which girls in particular will enjoy. RA 9+/IL 10-14

Tell the Moon to Come Out

Joan Lingard

Puffin £4.99 ISBN: 0 14 131689 6

It is 1936: Spain is being torn apart by bloody civil war. Nick is desperate to find his father, who left his Scottish family three years before to fight for the republican cause. Nick, who has to take the risk of travelling without papers, has been warned to trust no-one in this country where brother has betrayed brother. When he falls ill, Nick is forced to stop his search, but then an offer of help comes from an unexpected source.

This is a story about danger, trust and love that will keep you on the edge of your seat. RA 10+/IL 9-14

Secrets

Jacqueline Wilson, illustrated by Nick Sharratt

Corgi Yearling £4.99 ISBN: 0 440 86508 5

Posh India and streetwise Treasure forge a friendship based on a shared secret – they lead unhappy lives with inadequate parents. India's designer mother wants her to be thin, while Treasure is ill-treated by her mother and bullying boyfriend.

When Treasure becomes distraught at the idea of returning home, India hides her in her attic, in the manner of her heroine Anne Frank. Following their discovery, they come to terms with their 'unsatisfactory' parents in new and positive ways.

This is Jacqueline Wilson at her best, exploring adolescent issues and parental neglect with empathy, sensitivity and humour. RA 10+/IL 10+

Crispin: The Cross of Lead

Avi

Simon & Schuster Children's Books £7.99
ISBN: 0 689 83774 7

'Asta's son' is falsely accused of theft, decreed an outlaw from his village and forced to run for his life following the death of his mother. He is also shocked to discover he has a real name – Crispin – which is a clue to the secret of his birth. When he becomes the servant of a jester, he also learns that respect for authority must be earned.

Avi creates an intriguing picture of both rural and urban medieval life in the England of Edward III, and explores issues of power and individual freedom. RA 10+/IL 10+

Books for Teenagers

There is often little to distinguish teenage books from adult fiction, and many of the titles in this final section could also be classified as adult reads.

These books often tackle sensitive and demanding issues, such as abuse, cloning, drugs, murder, racism and sexuality. Intellectually and emotionally challenging, they can help young people to develop understanding, maturity and judgement.

Fake ID

Hazel Edwards

Lothian £3.99 ISBN: 0 7344 0442 5

Zoe is a 15-year-old Australian girl who loves hockey. Due to family circumstances, she is left to deal with the aftermath of her gran's death without the support of her mother or other family members.

As a result of a message her gran has left, to be read after her death, Zoe embarks on a voyage of discovery. She uncovers unexpected facts about her gran's past, and begins to question her own identity in the process.

The themes of self-knowledge and independence in this story will appeal to early teenage readers. RA 10+/IL 11-15

Bootleg

Alex Shearer

Macmillan Children's Books £4.99 ISBN: 0 330 41562 X

The Good for You party has won the latest election and is forcing everyone to lead healthier lives. Its top priority is the eradication of chocolate. Smudger and Huntly, chocolate devotees, discover, with the help of an elderly shop owner, how to make chocolate; they become bootleggers, but it is a dangerous business, for there are chocolate detector vans, Chocolate Trooper police, re-education centres and spies everywhere.

This exciting story has obvious parallels with life in Nazi Germany or Stalinist Russia, and is a well-told and gripping thriller. RA 10+/IL 11-15

Blitzed

Robert Swindells, illustrated by Robin Lawrie

Corgi Yearling £4.99 ISBN: 0 440 86397 X

George is obsessed by World War Two ephemera and therefore gets very excited about the school trip to Eden Camp, a war museum.

When George reaches Hut Five, he takes the opportunity to show off his knowledge by telling everyone about the reconstruction of an air raid on a house. Suddenly, time slips and he finds himself in wartime London, caught up in the Blitz and experiencing for real the things he has only learned about in history. RA 10+/IL 11+

Rain

Paul May

Corgi Yearling £4.99 ISBN: 0 440 86515 8

Rain has never known her father and never been to school but has lived a full and exciting life travelling around in an old bus with her mum, Max, who is an artist.

When the bus breaks down and they are finally forced to settle in one place, Rain can at last fulfil her desire to go to school and satisfy her lust for learning – or so she thinks.

In a book which paints a rather unflattering picture of our education system, both in social and academic terms, Paul May explores the difficulties experienced by someone perceived as being different, and also the joy and anxiety of an only child/single parent relationship. An interesting, thought-provoking and original story.
RA 10+/IL 11+

The Dark Horse

Marcus Sedgwick

Dolphin £7.99 ISBN: 1 84255 215 5

This is a gripping tale of betrayal, magic and tribal conflict, reminiscent of the Norse sagas.

Mouse is a girl with a mysterious past and an uncanny ability to communicate with animals. Rescued from a pack of wolves some years before, she now lives happily with Sigurd, her adopted brother, in the village of Storn. Their peaceful lives are shattered when a sinister stranger arrives in the village and Mouse discovers a wooden box – both are harbingers of danger from both outside and inside the tribe.

This is a thrilling and challenging read with a strong sense of time and place.
RA 11+/IL 11+

Tithe

Holly Black

Simon & Schuster Children's Books £5.99
ISBN: 0 689 86042 0

As a child, Kaye took her faerie friends for granted. Dragged back into their world as an independent 16-year-old, she discovers that it is no longer friendly, and patrolled by two competing rulers. Kaye falls for the dangerous Roiben, but when she is chosen as the tithe – a sacrifice made by faerie courts to secure their subjects' loyalty – will Roiben save her?

Holly Black's contemporary urban-gothic version of the fairy tale remains true to tradition, using the form to explore Kaye's transition from childhood to adulthood.
RA 10+/IL 11+

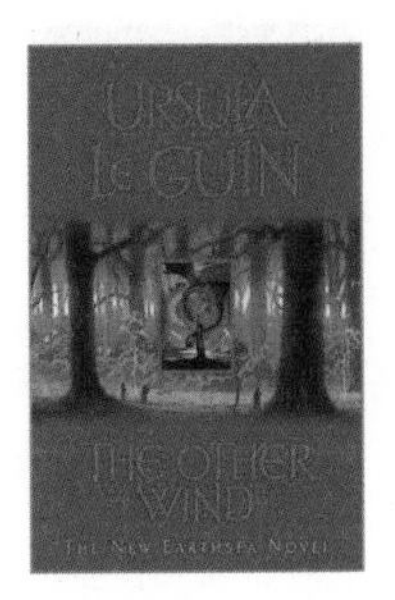

The Other Wind

Ursula Le Guin

Orion Children's Books £5.99 ISBN: 1 84255 211 2

Alder, an ordinary sorcerer, is haunted by nightmares about the world of the dead. He seeks help from Sparrowhawk, who recognises that Alder's suffering is connected with the reappearance of hostile dragons in the west. Alder joins Sparrowhawk's wife and daughter on their desperate quest to restore the old agreement between dragons and mankind, upon which Earthsea's equilibrium relies.

The Other Wind is a continuation of the *Chronicles of Earthsea*; it is also a luminous, absorbing meditation upon life, death and Man's relentless quest for immortality.
RA 11+/IL 10+

Child X

Lee Weatherly

Corgi £4.99 ISBN: 0 552 54800 6

It should be a great time for 14-year-old Jules, who has been given the leading role in a play. However, her adored father has discovered that Jules is not his child and is suing his wife for divorce and damages.

The misery of finding that he has apparently lost all his love for her is compounded by the media attention to which she and her mother are subjected, and the way in which, for legal reasons, she becomes 'Child X'.

In clean and convincing prose, Jules strongly communicates her love of acting and her complex feelings about her family and friends. RA 10+/IL 11-14

Keeper

Mal Peet

Walker Books £4.99 ISBN: 0 7445 9025 6

In this excellent football story, set in modern-day South America, a hackneyed football journalist sits down with El Gato (the Cat), a World Cup-winning goalkeeper, to look back on his amazing life and career.

The story begins in the jungle near El Gato's home town, and tells of his tough, early training with a mysterious former goalie on a ghostly, perfectly-cut pitch, surrounded by trees.

In addition to the moving story of El Gato's amazing rise to stardom from humble origins, *Keeper* has plenty of football action to keep enthusiasts of the game happy. RA 10+/IL 11+

Making Sense

Nadia Marks

Piccadilly Press £5.99 ISBN: 1 85340 748 8

What's it like to move to another country where everything seems strange and new? When Julia's family decides to relocate from Cyprus to London, she has to tackle this challenge first-hand.

Initially dazed and confused by English life, Julia gradually learns to find a new happiness in her adopted home, though she encounters many surprises and shocks along the way.

This good-hearted book realistically and humorously deals with the issue of fitting into a new culture, as well as exploring the wider pleasures and pains of growing up. RA 11+/IL 11+

Secret Sacrament

Sherryl Jordan

Simon & Schuster Children's Books £5.99
ISBN: 0 689 86045 5

Gabriel is haunted by an attack he witnesses on a Shinali tribeswoman by Navoran city soldiers. When his father dies, he defies family expectations and becomes a healer, learning skills from the Shinali. Soon, however, he is drawn into a power struggle between his Queen and her corrupt advisors and forced to flee for his life.

Gabriel is an attractive, believable character, facing complex situations as he negotiates his destiny through a wildly beautiful landscape. RA 11+/IL 11+

August '44

Carlo Gébler

Egmont £5.99 ISBN: 1 4052 0237 8

Before the war, Saul's father was a bullion dealer; now he is a homeless Jew, hiding in a cave with his family and friends, praying that the Allies will find them before the Germans.

Claude tries to ease the tension by telling Saul a story handed down to him by his Czech grandparents. This is the legend of the golem of Prague – a man made out of clay who was brought to life to help the Jewish community fight oppression.

Carlo Gébler's lively re-telling of the golem story underlines the long history of anti-Semitism in Europe and its devastating effect on one small boy caught up in the horror of World War Two. RA 11+/IL 11+

Fleshmarket

Nicola Morgan

Hodder Children's Books £5.99 ISBN: 0 340 85557 6

When Essie and Robbie's mother dies after an operation, they are abandoned by their father and left to fend for themselves in nineteenth-century Edinburgh. Robbie becomes mixed up in the sinister dealings of Burke and Hare (who provide doctors with bodies for research), but risks losing everything he holds dear.

Nicola Morgan's historical novel, based on real people, leaves us in no doubt about the debt we owe both to pioneering surgeons and the patients who allowed themselves to be operated on without anaesthetic. RA 10+/IL 12+

Fat Boy Swim

Catherine Forde

Egmont £4.99 ISBN: 1 4052 0239 4

Jimmy is overweight and bullied mercilessly wherever he goes, but he has a secret: he is a brilliant cook. Father Joseph wants a favour from Jimmy, but he won't accept it until he can help Jimmy get fit. Eventually, realising that he's got to take control of himself, Jimmy asks Joe to teach him to swim. He turns out to be a natural swimmer and commands respect in the pool, but he also has other demons to confront.

Although it contains distressing accounts of bullying, this story, set in Glasgow, is full of the complexities of human emotion. RA 10+/IL 12+

Pictures from the Fire

Gaye Hiçyilmaz

Dolphin £4.99 ISBN: 1 85881 896 6

Emilia, a Romanian Gypsy girl, is imprisoned in a room in a European hostel by her refugee parents, who blame her for the race riot that caused them to leave the UK.

This subtly-written sequel to *Girl in Red* gives new perspectives on the earlier novel, but is also a story in its own right, concentrating on the two threats to Emilia's freedom: her misogynistic, aloof, but disenfranchised parents, and the hatred brought about by racism.

Although the book is clearly an indictment of racism, it also suggests that the integration of cultures cannot be one-sided and that refugees must embrace the new societies in which they find themselves. RA 11+/IL 11+

Guitar Girl

Sarra Manning

Hodder Children's Books £5.99 ISBN: 0 340 86071 5

17-year-old Molly and her two friends dream of starting a girl band and singing about ordinary things, such as school and those little toys you get in plastic eggs. After their first 'official' gig, they are approached by Dean and T, who offer to join the band and help them find stardom.

Molly is plunged into the terrifying world of celebrity, which leaves her struggling to remember who she was before she became lead singer of *The Hormones*.

Sarra Manning tells the story in an approachable way, perfectly portraying the mood swings of the teenage girls. RA 10+/IL 12+

Angel: Haggis Horrors and Heavenly Bodies

Cherry Whytock

Piccadilly Press £5.99 ISBN: 1 85340 713 5

Angel Potts is not a typical teenager: she has fabulously wealthy and eccentric parents and lives around the corner from Harrods. Despite this, Angel has most of the same worries and concerns of many teens: embarrassing parents, spots, boys, and an obsession with her image and food.

In this book, Angel's father is arrested when he protests against Harrods' haggis; her best friend goes to live in the USA; and her mates rally round to uncover a dastardly fraud. It is very, very funny – a delightfully stress-free read that teenagers (and their parents) will love. RA 11+/IL 12+

The Oracle

Catherine Fisher

Hodder Children's Books £5.99 ISBN: 0 340 84376 4

Mirany is the new Bearer, risking her life to perform the dangerous rituals of the Oracle, a God in whom she has no belief. The God lives in the Archon, who must give up his life in the hope that his death will bring rain to the parched land and save his people. Just before he dies the Archon passes a note to Mirany; she soon finds herself involved with a drunken musician, corruption in high places and the search for the new Archon.

This is an intriguing and atmospheric fantasy, encompassing themes of belief, loyalty and friendship. RA 11+/IL 12+

Firesong

William Nicholson

Egmont £6.99 ISBN: 1 4052 0654 3

Firesong is the third volume in the *Wind on Fire* trilogy. The Manth people have escaped from the Mastery and must confront many dangers before finally reaching their homeland.

Bowman and Kestrel face an awesome responsibility for the future of their people: they must unravel the mysteries of the Singer people and prepare to face their worst fears.

William Nicholson has a real gift for characterisation and storytelling, but his imaginative and gripping fantasy also tackles serious issues concerning the misuse of power and the consequences of greed and cruelty. RA 11+/IL 12+

Dead Gorgeous

Malorie Blackman

Corgi £4.99 ISBN: 0 552 54633 X

Nova is bored and discontented, largely ignored by her harassed, overworked, hotel-owning parents, and jealous of her older sister's skinny figure. When she meets the good-looking Liam, she can't believe her luck, but then she discovers that he is not quite like other boys.

In this unusual ghost story Malorie Blackman provides a many-layered account of the causes and effects of parental neglect and sibling rivalry, and ultimately offers hope to readers experiencing the trauma of adolescent isolation. RA 11+/IL 12+

Martyn Pig

Kevin Brooks

The Chicken House £5.99 ISBN: 1 903434 99 8

Martyn Pig leads a fairly dismal life, living alone with his drunken, abusive father. During a violent outburst, Martyn pushes his dad in self-defence and accidentally kills him. When his friendly neighbour, Alex, discovers his awful secret, she takes charge, helping him to dispose of the body, and entangling Martyn in an increasingly complicated web of deceit.

In his debut novel, Kevin Brooks successfully combines suspense, humour, and an unexpected twist, to create a darkly-comic thriller that will grip readers right up to the final page. RA 11+/IL 12+

Kissing Vanessa

Simon Cheshire

Piccadilly Press £5.99 ISBN: 1 85340 723 2

Kevin has fallen in love with the new girl in his class: she's beautiful, charming and shares his hobby, photography. But Kevin feels he's not very successful at attracting girls and Vanessa doesn't seem to be smitten by him, so he goes to his friend Jack for advice.

Jack is writing a book, *Girlfriend Management the Easy Way*, but following his advice turns out to have disastrous, if highly amusing, results. RA 11+/IL 12+

Coraline

Neil Gaiman, illustrated by Dave McKean

Bloomsbury Children's Books £5.99 ISBN: 0 7475 6210 5

One day Coraline unlocks a mysterious door that opens on to another world, a twisted parody of Coraline's own dimension. She discovers something very sinister about her 'other mother', who has trapped her real parents and plans to keep the family there forever. As Coraline tries to escape, she is faced with a fantastical series of macabre and bizarre situations.

Excellently written, and superbly original, *Coraline* is well-suited to those who enjoy reading about the weird and the wonderful with a dash of horror and humour.
RA 11+/IL 12+

All American Girl

Meg Cabot

Macmillan Children's Books £5.99 ISBN: 0 330 41555 7

Teenager Sam is the All American Girl of the title, a privileged youngster with caring parents and two sisters, living in comfortable, middle-class Washington D.C. One day, she just happens to save the life of the President. This brings her instant fame and changes her life in ways she never imagined; in the process she learns a lot about herself and those around her.

This very 'girly' book is full of talk about clothes, hairstyles and pop stars, but it also tackles the serious issues of loyalty and consideration for others. Fluffy and fun.
RA 12+/IL 12+

Ryland's Footsteps

Sally Prue

Oxford University Press £4.99 ISBN: 0 19 275339 8

Rye moves to an island penal colony when his father, a cloning scientist, is appointed Governor. He befriends Kris – son of the native people's chief, who wants to preserve the old ways – and Stefanie, daughter of a prison inmate accused of fomenting revolution. Rye is fearful of becoming like his father, a fear that is fully justified when he learns that he is his father's clone.

A powerful and, at times, darkly-humorous story, which raises topical themes.
RA 12+/IL 12+

What's Your Problem?

Bali Rai

Barrington Stoke £4.99 ISBN 1 84299 126 4

Jaspal, born and brought up in Leicester, is 14 when his father moves the family to rural Nottinghamshire for a 'better life'. However, they soon become targets for racial abuse, hate mail and threats. Jaspal is victimised by Steggsy and his gang for being the only non-white at his school, but, in spite of ignorance and prejudice, Jaspal makes friends and enjoys his lessons.

However, when he beats Steggsy in a fight, matters take an ugly turn with tragic consequences. The conflicts and tensions in Jaspal's life are movingly described in this compelling, yet disturbing, story for reluctant older readers. RA 9+/IL 12+

Borderland

Rhiannon Lassiter

Oxford University Press £4.99 ISBN: 0 19 275237 5

Zoe, who wants to fit in at school, is delighted when she is befriended by Laura. However, she is in for a shock: Laura and her brother Alex take her through a secret door to another world – Shattershard. Here, Alex is the leader of the Hajhim, a terrorist group that intends to destroy the city; Laura, posing as a merchant, is his spy.

As Zoe becomes drawn into their activities, she questions their involvement in this other world. This exciting and enjoyable story raises serious political issues, but has spirited characters and a good plot. RA 12+/IL 12+

Caught in the Crossfire

Alan Gibbons

Dolphin £4.99 ISBN: 1 84255 096 9

Oakfield is a town of white and Asian ghettos. The Patriotic Party wants a whites-only England and to this end incites race war. On different sides of the line are the Khans and the Kellys; Liam Kelly finds fulfilment in the Patriotic Party while Tahir Khan believes all whites are racist.

Their siblings Rabir and Mike begin dating, but it is difficult for them to find anywhere to meet without provoking hostility from one family or the other. These are serious and thought-provoking themes in a pacily-written and dramatic novel. RA 12+/IL 12+

The Folk Keeper

Franny Billingsley

Bloomsbury Children's Books £5.99 ISBN: 0 7475 6054 4

The Folk are wild beasts that wreak havoc on the human world. A strange and ungainly orphan, Corinna Stonewall, would seem an unlikely candidate for the position of Folk Keeper, but, when she accepts, she has no idea that her new appointment will unlock the key to understanding who she really is.

Corinna initially comes across as cold and barely human, but as she discovers more about herself – and begins to fall in love – she becomes a warmer and more sympathetic character. The prose is beautiful, lyrical and surprising. RA 12+/IL 12+

Blue Moon

Julia Green

Puffin £4.99 ISBN: 0 141 31535 0

Mia is 15 years old and pregnant. She skips school, getting further behind in her GCSE work. When Dad finally finds out he is furious; he arranges an abortion but at the last minute Mia runs away from the hospital, determined to keep the baby. On the run, and in the company of strangers, she is forced to evaluate what really matters to her.

This tense, moving story, with its finely drawn characters, draws us into Mia's dilemma, engaging us as she flounders, half-woman, half-child, in a sea of troubles. RA 10+/IL 13+

Malarkey

Keith Gray

Red Fox £4.99 ISBN: 0 09 943944 1

Within a few hours of starting at a new school, John Malarkey, a strong-minded teenager, is accused of a theft he did not commit. As he tries to sort out the problem and deal with the pupils who used him as a scapegoat, he gets himself into much deeper trouble.

John's struggle to prove his innocence and smash the gang (which is, in effect, controlling the school) is recounted in gritty language, and the last chapter provides a dramatic conclusion to a powerful story line that is not afraid to confront the horrors of bullying and blackmail. RA 11+ /IL 13+

Starseeker

Tim Bowler

Oxford University Press £5.99 ISBN: 0 19 275305 3

Luke used to be a studious boy, engrossed in his piano-playing, but since his father died, and his mother started a new relationship, he has become obsessed with proving himself as a member of Skin's gang. Gradually, however, he begins to realise that he has been granted the very special gift of being able to interpret life itself, and as a result takes life-changing decisions.

Tim Bowler's powerful novel considers profound questions (abstract philosophical and religious theories; the psychological effects of loss; rights and responsibilities) all set within a pacy and exciting thriller saturated with teenage angst. RA 11+/IL 13+

Sorceress

Celia Rees

Bloomsbury Children's Books £5.99 ISBN: 0 7475 5568 0

Accused of witchcraft, Mary flees from the Puritan settlement of Beulah into the icy wastes of the New World. She is rescued by Native Americans and begins a new life of happiness and tragedy, magic and healing. Agnes, a descendent of Mary, feels compelled to track Mary's life through the events of the seventeenth century, and in the process finds her own place in today's world.

This enthralling and moving sequel to *Witch Child* is also a well-written and satisfying read in its own right. RA 11+/IL 13+

Friction

E. R. Frank

Simon & Schuster Children's Books £8.99
ISBN: 0 689 83749 6

Simon is a great teacher who is loved by every pupil in his class, especially Alex and her best friend Tim. Suddenly a new girl, Stacy, begins to insinuate that Simon is a pervert and that his behaviour towards Alex is highly suspect.

These poisonous rumours infect everyone and cause friction between friends. But are they true?

This a disturbing and, in parts, explicit story about the complex nature of truth and lies and the impact they can have on people's lives. RA 11+/IL 13+

Coming of Age

Valerie Mendes

Simon & Schuster Children's Books £8.99
ISBN: 0 689 83716 X

Amy loses her memory of witnessing the riding accident in which her mother was killed. Years later, as she is about to turn 16, Amy's life again changes dramatically; her father, the centre of her life, wants to re-marry.

When she stumbles across evidence that her mother's death may not have been an accident, Amy sets out to uncover the truth. Gradually she comes to realise that growing up means letting go of old ideas and perceptions. RA 12+/IL 13+

No Shame, No Fear

Ann Turnbull

Walker Books £5.99 ISBN: 0 7445 9090 6

Susanna's Quaker family face persecution in a post-Civil War England still divided by religion. With her father in prison, Susanna starts a new life working for a printer. William, an Anglican, works in his family's business. A chance meeting draws Will to Susanna and her quiet, steady faith, but he must defy his father in order to help Susanna defend her beliefs.

The narrative deftly reveals the complex dilemmas faced by ordinary people in the wake of war. This is a pleasingly unexpected take on the boy-meets-girl romance, set in a fascinating historical context. RA 12+/IL 13+

Feed

M. T. Anderson

Walker Books £4.99 ISBN: 0 7445 9085 X

In the future people will have 'feeds' implanted into their heads, which will supply the addicted users with a never-ending babble of entertainment.

Titus falls for Violet, a girl he meets on the moon. When their feeds are sabotaged, they recover, feed-free, in a hospital. Titus's feed is repaired and he returns to his feed-dependent self; Violet's implant, however, continues to malfunction and her interconnected life support system begins to fail.

This is a witty Orwellian satire on consumerism gone mad, written in a highly original style. RA 12+/IL 13+

Last Seen Wearing Trainers

Rosie Rushton

Andersen Press £5.99 ISBN: 1 84270 216 5

When Katie meets a dashing young stranger called Joe, she feels that life may finally be taking a turn for the better. Her autistic brother has become increasingly dependent on her, her mother is drinking excessively and her father's death still haunts the family. When Joe suggests she teach them a lesson by running away with him, she finds herself willingly complying.

The book follows the family's reactions to the teenager's disappearance, as well as Katie's own increasing sense of unease and fear, as the awful nature of Joe's hidden agenda becomes apparent. A gripping, emotionally-charged thriller. RA 12+/IL 13+

Now That I've Found You

Rex Harley

Pont Books £4.99 ISBN: 1 84323 107 7

The teenage boy who narrates this spellbinding novel falls in love with a most unusual girl: she dresses and acts as if she lives in 1968, has old money in her pockets, is mesmerised by cars, and has never heard of a CD. But what is the reason behind this eccentricity.

This original and thought-provoking book has a complex and well-plotted narrative that builds up layer upon layer of understanding as the reader discovers more about the pasts of the two fascinating central characters. RA 12+/IL 13+

Fake

K. K. Beck

Scholastic Point £4.99 ISBN: 0 439 98207 3

'Problem teenagers' Danny and Keith escape from the 'brat camp' to which they have been sent. Keith, who is not all he seems, hijacks Danny's identity; Danny, meanwhile, adopts an amnesiac identity and is taken care of by elderly Olive, who shows him that not all adults are selfish or inadequate and that facing up to who you are is the only true way forward. And Keith? What becomes of him?

This is a gripping page-turner that keeps you guessing until the last sentence. RA 12+/IL 13+

The Shell House

Linda Newbery

Red Fox £5.99 ISBN: 0 099 45593 5

The Shell House of the title is Graveney Hall, a beautiful home that burned down during the First World War. It links the stories of Greg, who is photographing the hall for his 'A' level project, and Edmund, the Graveney family's last heir, who disappeared mysteriously in 1917.

Greg feels increasingly guilty about rejecting the tentative advances of his male friend Jordan, and is concerned that an argument with his friend Faith has caused her to lose her Christian belief. Edmund's story is also overshadowed by religious intolerance and homosexuality.

This is a beautifully written and thought-provoking novel. RA 12+/IL 13+

Knife Edge

Sylvia Hall

Scholastic Point £4.99 ISBN: 0 439 97816 5

David is convinced that his mum was murdered by his dad, and is determined to avenge her death at any cost. Sent to live with sympathetic foster parents, who hope thereby to overcome their own family loss, he feels unable to allow himself to grieve, accept love and sympathy, or allow anyone else to bring his father to justice.

Readers of this searching psychological novel, told in a colloquial first-person present tense, will be engaged, horrified and, ultimately, relieved as the story moves towards its resolution. RA 10+/IL 14+

The Earth, My Butt and Other Big, Round Things

Carolyn Mackler

Walker Books £5.99 ISBN: 0 7445 9077 9

Virginia misses her best friend Shannon and is dissatisfied at being the only one in the family who is not slim, clever or successful. To compensate, she comfort-eats. In spite of her attempts to diet, events conspire against her when her adored brother Byron is suspended from college in disgrace. Virginia, seizing the opportunity to get away from the gloom of home, begins to view herself differently.

This is a well-written and positive story about negotiating the difficult ways of being one's self. RA 11+/IL 14+

Babyshoes

Dawn Garisch

Simon & Schuster £8.99 ISBN: 0 689 83711 9

18-year-old David helps deliver his baby brother, so when his mother leaves home and boyfriend Trevor threatens to put baby Kevin in care, David decides to seek out his own father, taking with him his guitar, his best friend Rudd – and baby Kevin!

This humorous coming-of-age novel, set in South Africa, explores from David's viewpoint what it is like to juggle work, surrogate fatherhood, falling in love (with mother and daughter!) and building family relationships. The large typeset should add appeal for reluctant readers. RA 11+/IL 14+

The Moon Riders

Theresa Tomlinson

Corgi £5.99 ISBN: 0 552 54910 X

Myrina is a young girl in the nomadic Mazagardi tribe, who joins the Moon Riders, a group of Amazonian women warriors. Myrina learns how to use medicinal herbs, perform the sacred Moon dances and fight on horseback, against the backdrop of the build-up to the Trojan War. Myrina matures into a brave and fierce warrior, using her strength to fight for Troy against Achilles and the Acheans.

This is an exciting, action-packed retelling of the story of the Trojan War, with an interesting twist and a powerful cast of female characters. RA 11+/IL 14+

The Queen of Everything

Deb Caletti

Scholastic Point £4.99 ISBN: 0 439 97699 5

Jordan leads a typical American teenage life (divorced parents, stepfamily, weekend job, boyfriend, best friend). Into her father's life walks charismatic Gayle, who is perfect, but married. Life unravels in an alarming way as Jordan's safe, predictable father begins a passionate affair. Jordan's own ideas about love and loyalty to her boyfriend are challenged as she develops a relationship with a loner.

A perceptive, funny, shocking and completely engrossing teenage read, told in Jordan's riveting and acutely self-aware narrative voice. RA 11+/IL 14+

Waking Dream

Rhiannon Lassiter

Macmillan Children's Books £4.99 ISBN: 0 330 39701 X

This is the story of three cousins: Poppy, Bethany and Rivalaum. Their parents have hidden an incredible secret from them for many years: each of their fathers came from the land of Dream.

When Bethany's father dies he leaves her a mysterious painting of a landscape. As the cousins begin to visit the same landscape in their dreams, they are inexorably drawn into a quest to find the truth about themselves.

This is a densely-layered novel, full of references to poetry and literature and the

I is Someone Else

Patrick Cooper

Andersen Press £5.99 ISBN: 1 84270 306 4

On a French exchange trip in 1966, 15-year-old Stephen meets two strangers on the ferry: glamorous Astrid and her laid-back boyfriend Jerry. When it transpires that they know his missing older brother, last seen in Istanbul, Stephen joins them on a dangerous journey through central Asia to India. He encounters drugs and girls, and experiences friendship and betrayal, all of which force him to confront his own terrible secret.

This well-crafted novel tackles the confused sexuality of a teenage boy sensitively, as well as capturing the spirit of the 1960s. RA 11+/IL 14+

One Night

Margaret Wild

Allen & Unwin £5.99 ISBN: 1 86508 928 1

Margaret Wild's verse is pithy and accessible; her characterisation is meticulous and her plots race along without becoming bogged down by lengthy descriptive passages.

In *One Night*, a series of short poems brings a number of perspectives to a story about three troubled teenagers, who have developed different strategies for coping with the pain of life: Al is a binge drinker, Bram organises wild parties and Gabe has a string of sexual partners, one of whom, Helen, gets pregnant. This sparks a chain of events that culminates in the young men addressing the troubles in their lives. RA 11+/IL 14+

What the Birds See

Sonya Hartnett

Walker Books £7.99 ISBN: 0 7445 9093 0

Adrian is 'a child for whom life easily falls apart', a nine-year-old who is afraid of almost everything and has never known his father. Because his mother is too ill to care for him, he lives with his grandmother – who feels she cannot give him what he needs – and an uncle who never leaves the house.

This is a beautifully written novel, which is nevertheless difficult to enjoy, as it is so suffused with unhappiness from beginning to end. As such, it is a disturbing read, suitable only for older children and adults. RA 11+/IL 14+

Family Break-up and Step-families

Fantasy

Friendship

if you care about the books that children read ...

why not visit our specialist children's book website

www.booktrusted.com

where teachers, librarians, parents and readers can find information about:

- books for all ages
- news and events
- children's book prizes
- specialist bookshops
- web resources

You can also find out about children's book illustrators and view examples of their work at our new online gallery of illustrators.

So if you care about the books that children read ...
www.booktrusted.com